PINNACLE

How to Land the Right Job and Find Fulfillment in Your Career

GERALD WALSH

ISBN 978-0-9949636-0-4 (Print version)
ISBN 978-0-9949636-1-1 (ePub)
ISBN 978-0-9949636-2-8 (PDF)

Published by:
Gerald Walsh Associates Inc.
Halifax, Canada

For more information about career coaching and public speaking, or to order additional copies of this book, pleased contact:

Gerald Walsh Associates Inc.
(902) 421-1676

Or visit our website
www.GeraldWalsh.com

TABLE OF CONTENTS

Introduction

SECTION 1: THE PLAN

SECTION 2: THE TOOLBOX

SECTION 3: THE SEARCH

SECTION 4: THE INTERVIEW

SECTION 5: THE OFFER

SECTION 6: THE NEW JOB

ACKNOWLEDGEMENTS

ABOUT THE AUTHOR

Introduction

- Are you happy in your career?
- Do you wake up every morning looking forward to going to work?
- Is the work you do interesting and challenging?
- Are you spending time at work with people you like and bosses you respect?
- Are you being paid fairly for your efforts?
- Are you proud to tell your friends and family who you work for and what you do?
- Does your employer offer you the opportunity to learn and advance?
- Do your values align with your employer's values?
- Do you feel energized at the end of a work day?

The odds are that you have answered '*no*' to all or at least several of these questions.

But consider for a moment. What would it feel like to be able to answer '*yes*' to every one of those questions? What would it feel like if your work was like play: something you looked forward to doing? What would it feel like if you were at the top of your game all the time and the envy of your peers, family and friends?

This book can help you get there.

That's because the principles that I will share with you apply universally to anybody looking to get the most out of their career. Whether you are a young professional still trying to get launched on the right career path, at mid-career and hoping to advance your career, or at late-career and seeking meaningful work in the last phase of your career, *PINNACLE: How to Land the Right Job and Find Fulfillment in Your Career* will help you find meaning, fun and fair pay from your career.

How do I do this?

I have been an executive recruiter for over 25 years. During those years, I have completed thousands of searches at the management and professional levels, placing individuals in key positions like Chief Executive Officer, President, Vice President, General Manager, Executive Director, Chief Administrative

Officer, and so on. I have also successfully placed individuals in more junior positions such as Business Analyst, Marketing Coordinator, Customer Service Representatives, Executive Assistant, Human Resource Assistant, and others.

The organizations that use my services include major corporations, owner-managed businesses, not-for-profit associations, governments and NGOs. Over those years, they have entrusted me with the important task of finding great people for their organizations. In turn, I take very seriously the business of advising them on the type of people to hire.

In doing these searches, I have personally interviewed more than 10,000 people. Yes, 10,000 individuals who have taken me into their confidence and shared valuable and personal information with me about their careers and their lives. I've learned what's worked and not worked for them throughout their careers. Now I want to share this experience with you.

How my own career has influenced this book

Like so many things in life, including careers, success is a combination of talent, effort and good fortune (otherwise known as "luck"). This formula certainly applies to me and it has radically altered my thinking about the role of people in making any business successful.

After finishing my MBA, I joined a small dental supply business as its controller, even though I didn't know that much about accounting. I mention this job because in hindsight it was one of my smartest career moves, although I didn't realize it at the time. You see, working for a small company, especially early in your career, gives you the opportunity to experience things you would never experience in a larger company. The owner put me in charge (at 23 years of age) of the accounting department where I managed a staff of five people, dealt with the company's banker and outside accountant, managed the cash flow, and generally oversaw anything related to finances. No big company would have given me that level of responsibility at such a young age.

(I recommend this strategy of working for a small company to any young person hoping to kick start their career. The experience you will get is invaluable as it will give you the opportunity to do things you would never get to do otherwise.)

The coffee break story

After working for a few years in the dental supply business and obtaining my CPA professional accounting designation, I started to get impatient and began my search for another job. During my search, I came across two good opportunities, both paying roughly the same salary. One was as a commercial banker, lending to mid-sized businesses, and the other was a finance manager role with a major telecommunications company. Looking back, it's interesting to see how career decisions are influenced.

I can recall being interviewed one morning at the head office of the telecommunications company. The interview was going well and I liked the people who were interviewing me. I could sense that they also liked me and were interested in having me join them.

But something happened that morning that turned me off to that opportunity. What happened was that at 10:15 am, the entire department got up from their desks and en masse marched out the door to go on their 15-minute coffee break. It was just like the fire alarm had rung and everybody was marching dutifully to the exit.

What I discovered about myself from observing this mass exodus for coffee is that I wouldn't do well in a culture that is so rigid and so rule-bound. I wanted more autonomy from my work. I didn't want to be part of an army. So I chose the commercial banking option.

I tell that story when I speak to groups of people about job searching because it is an example of the importance of observing the culture of an organization when you are going through the interview process. Let's face it: Interviews are a bit artificial, in that everybody is on their best behaviour, trying to make a favourable impression on the other. As a job candidate, there are few chances to find out what an employer is really like. So, watch for those small clues that can reveal a lot about corporate culture and working conditions.

Commercial banking was a great experience for me as it exposed me to dealing directly with customers for the first time in my career. I loved the process of prospecting for new business and putting together deals for clients. I learned what it was like to negotiate on behalf of the bank and to discover just how strategic a good negotiator has to be. I experienced the thrill of closing a transaction knowing that I had done a good job on behalf of the bank and that the customer was happy too. And on top of all that I was still using my accounting skills, albeit in a very different way.

Paul's story

Banking also inadvertently exposed me to another matter that I hadn't given much thought to before then: the importance of taking charge of your own career and not relying on your employer to do it.

I sat next to another banker whose name was Paul (not his real name.) Paul had joined the bank when he was eighteen years old, straight out of high school. He was then 48 years old meaning he had thirty years in with the bank by that time. The problem was that Paul absolutely hated his job and could not wait until retirement, which was still at least another seven years away. Paul also had the tendency to talk about his frustration often, almost every day, to those around him, including me.

You may ask: *why didn't Paul go find another job somewhere?* That's the problem. He couldn't. Paul's frustration was driven by the fact that he had no real options other than to stay in banking. If you looked at Paul's situation here's what you saw:

- No formal education beyond high school.
- Weak technology skills that were limited only to the bank's software.
- A limited network of contacts, because he had transferred a lot with the bank and never stayed in one location long enough to build a good network.
- A job that paid way more than he was really worth "on the street," in other words, way more than he could earn elsewhere.
- An excellent range of health benefits that he couldn't afford to give up.
- A pension that was going to pay him about 70% of his pay in his retirement years, if he lived that long!

On top of all this, Paul's health had deteriorated over the years and he was overweight with high blood pressure. When you looked at the world from Paul's eyes, you could easily understand why he was so stressed. The world looked pretty bleak to him at the time because he felt he had no alternatives.

Not surprisingly, Paul went on to have a nervous breakdown not long after I joined the bank. Fortunately that scare was enough to cause him to change his ways and realize that he could have a life outside banking. He retired early, accepted a reduced pension and established himself as a self-employed investment advisor, where he could set his own hours and earn a living based on his own performance. With the support of his family, he was able to reduce his living expenses considerably and not worry so much about money.

When I last saw Paul (on a golf course, coincidently) his health had improved and he was very happy with his lot in life. He said to me that his only regret is that he hadn't made the change years earlier.

What I took from this, as still a relatively young guy at the time, was that I always needed to have career options available to me. That meant if I ever got fired or decided that I could not stand my employer and wanted to leave, I could find a comparable job with relative ease. I knew I had to keep my contacts current, my skills up to date, and I had to have confidence that my experience was meaningful and saleable to another employer.

In hindsight, working with Paul taught me this important career lesson, one I am grateful for and that could be followed by everybody.

––––––––––

While my career with the bank continued to flourish, I became more and more drawn to running my own business. Then, an opportunity literally fell into my lap. With a couple of other people, I began discussing the idea of opening my own human resources firm focusing on executive search. Even though I knew next to nothing about human resources, having worked my entire career so far in accounting and finance, I believed that I could transition into a role like that, particularly after learning about business to business selling through banking. And so 25 years ago, I took the plunge and started my own executive search business. Nine years later, I bought out my partners and have been 100% owner of the firm ever since.

Until this point, I thought management was all about the numbers. I thought that because I had an MBA, I could just sit in my office, with spreadsheets of numbers laid out in front of me and make decisions based on what those numbers said. It didn't matter how those decisions affected people or customers. You did what the numbers dictated.

While that type of thinking may seem silly now, my MBA training did reinforce it. I had been taught that for the most part, management was a science. (In fact, I am pretty sure there was a course called Management Science in our program.) These courses taught us that organizational decisions could be reduced to a set of formulae, programs and methodologies that could be applied to all types of decisions.

While I respect the value in number crunching and have a decent aptitude for numbers, I began to realize this type of thinking was wrong and that real value for any organization was in its people and how well they performed, not on how well someone "does the numbers."

At the same time, I also grew to appreciate the importance of 'fit' especially for knowledge-based workers. Some companies value and seek low-skilled, low-paid, highly-productive employees (like cogs in a machine, if you will) that results in more profit for the company. In these companies if you show up on time, keep your head down and do your work, you will be rewarded with a salary and maybe some benefits. If you don't perform this way you can easily be replaced.

But for knowledge-based workers, the goal is often different. They want to find careers where the work is meaningful, where ideas are sought and valued, where their values and those of their employer align, and where the pay is fair. This is where 'fit' comes into the hiring equation and it is something both the employer and you should be thinking about when interviewing for a job.

It is also why we, at Gerald Walsh Associates, say our mission is: *To help organizations find the right people and help individuals find the right careers.*

How this book is organized

I know that the process of figuring out what you should do and then getting there will not be easy. As you can see, my path started in business and accounting and ended up in human resources, in fact, being self-employed in human resources. I am very happy doing what I do as it feels like I am making a contribution to other people's lives and helping organizations succeed.

I am fortunate it turned out the way it has for me. But the path may not be as easy for you. That is why I have written this book as if you have a career coach by your side every step of the way. The book is full of exercises that you should do as you go through each chapter. It's a hands-on book that requires work on your part in order to achieve your career goals. In other words, you have to be a participant, not a spectator. I strongly encourage you to take your time and complete each exercise as you go through the chapters.

Finding the right career is also a process that should be approached in a logical, orderly manner. For example, it makes no sense to worry about your interviewing technique until you have a clear understanding of the type of job you want and the type of organization you want to work for. That's why I have organized this book so that it describes the job search process chronologically in six sections:

Section One: The Plan

This is arguably the most critical part of the job search process because it sets the stage for everything that follows, and helps you find the right direction for you. All too often, people come to me wondering if their resume should be three pages or two pages, or to help them prepare for an upcoming interview. I like to ask them a simple question: *What kind of job are you looking for?* The majority of people would not have a clear answer to that question. You absolutely must have a good understanding of the type of job that will make you happy. Otherwise, you run a high risk of taking the wrong job. That's why having meaningful career goals is so important before you embark on your search. This section will help you build that plan.

Section Two: The Toolbox

Before beginning your search, you will need a complete set of tools at your disposal. If these are not sharp, you will not be able to get the job done. The basic tools you need are: a resume that identifies your education, work experience and accomplishments; a cover letter that explains why you are a suitable candidate for the job and links your background to the potential employer's needs; a list of references who will say good things about you; and a social media presence that leaves a positive impression in the eyes of anyone who checks on you. This book will give you all the tools you need.

Section Three: The Search

In this section, you will learn the mechanics of conducting a job search. For most people this is the hardest and most intimidating step, because you will be forced to deal with rejection, probably more than once. But don't worry: that's part of the process and your skin will thicken over time.

To help you conduct an efficient and thorough search, we will focus on the four ways to find a job: using your personal connections to generate job leads, connecting with employers directly, establishing relationships with professional recruiters and employment agencies and responding to publicized job openings.

Section Four: The Interview

For many people, the interview is the most important step in the job search process. It is, after all, the point when a potential employer decides if you are the right person for them. It's also the time when you decide if the job is right for you.

This section contains dozens of tips that will remove any anxiety you have about being interviewed and replace that with knowledge, skill and confidence that you can apply in every interview situation. You will learn what to do to get ready for the interview, everything from anticipating the questions you will be asked to deciding what to wear, what to expect during the interview so nothing takes you by surprise, and what you can do after the interview is over to leave a great final impression.

Section Five: The Offer

This is the fun part of the job search process: when weeks or months of writing cover letters, preparing resumes, networking with employers and going through interviews finally pays off – a new employer wants you to join them. But with this excitement comes the anxiety and nervousness that comes with a big decision. Will this be the right move for you? Can you negotiate a good salary? Will you like your new co-workers? What will your current employer say when you resign? Should you just stay where you are?

In this section, you will learn how to evaluate job offers objectively, determine what you are worth, negotiate "like a pro" so that you end up with the best possible package and learn the best way to resign your current job so that you do not burn any bridges when leaving for a new job.

Section Six: The New Job

A career change cannot be considered complete until you have successfully integrated into the new job. The first year is a particularly challenging time as you meet new people, learn new processes, build new skills, and adapt to an entirely new work environment. Many people do not make it through the first year or if they do, they often find the new role is not what they had hoped for. Some people even return to their old jobs. In this section of the book, we will identify simple strategies you can follow to make your career change complete and successful.

Throughout many of the chapters, you will find stories of real career challenges faced by people just like you. Each of these individuals has graciously offered to write or tell me their own story and describe their own situation. In some cases, the person is identified; in other cases, the person wished to remain anonymous. These stories will help you realize that you are not alone in the job search process. Others have faced similar circumstances and this alone should give you a boost of confidence.

I have also included a section called "Ask Gerry" throughout the book. These are real questions I have been asked over the years and I am confident my answers to these questions will add to your knowledge about job searching and your confidence on the journey.

The principles and practices I have laid out in this book will help you find a job you love. All you have to do is stay focused, manage your time wisely and enjoy the fulfilling career you are creating. Let's get started.

Section One

The Plan

**"Whether you think you can or
you think you can't, you're probably right"**

- Henry Ford

Chapter 1

Can You Afford To Follow Your Passion?

"All you need in this life is ignorance and confidence; then success is sure."

- Mark Twain

IT'S HARD TO argue with Steve Jobs' success but he certainly sparked a hot debate with his follow-your-passion commencement speech to Stanford University graduates in 2005.

In that speech – which focused on three stories from Jobs' personal experience – he said, "Your work is going to fill a large part of your life and the only way to be truly satisfied is to do … great work. And the only way to do great work is to love what you do. If you haven't found it yet, keep looking, don't settle."

Some people will tell you that Jobs' proclamation of "keep looking, don't settle" has directed many young people into a life of underemployment while they sought the work they love. That's probably an overstatement, but it did start a worthwhile debate about whether "following your passion" is good career advice or not.

One thing is for certain: those who preach follow-your-passion are almost always people who took a risk and through a combination of hard work, determination, commitment, brains and luck, they achieved great success.

What you'll never see is the opposite. You won't hear the more frequent stories of people who followed their passion and failed. They certainly won't be telling you to follow in their footsteps. Dilbert creator, Scott Adams, the author of *How to Fail at Almost Everything and Still Win Big,* has an interesting spin on this subject – as only Dilbert could. He says successful people don't want to say they are smarter or more talented than the average person. That wouldn't sound good, even though it may be true. Instead, these very successful people usually say that passion for their work is their reason for success. It sounds plausible – but it implies that anybody can do it.

I don't doubt the sincerity of anyone who credits passion for work as their reason for success. But I can't help but wonder if this advice can inadvertently send people – especially young people – down the wrong path.

In fairness, how are you supposed to know if you will be happy as a graphic designer, teacher or banker if you haven't actually tried any of these careers yet?

Take, for example, a passionate amateur chef who loves cooking and hosting big dinner parties for friends. Is telling that person to follow her passion and open a restaurant good career advice?

Perhaps so – if it ends up that happy customers are lined up out the door, business is booming, and the owner is having fun.

On the other hand if the new owner finds herself working 18 hours a day, seven days a week and having difficulty attracting paying customers and good employees, there is a good chance that owner will lose her "passion" for cooking quickly.

Peter, a former sales rep in the restaurant supply business, summed it up well. He told me about a meeting he had with the director of the restaurant association. When Peter asked why restaurant start-ups and closures seemed so common, the director responded that when you ask aspiring restaurateurs why they want to open a restaurant, most would express their passion for cooking, their pride of owning a business, and their love for hospitality and serving people. Few, he said, had "considered accounting, business planning, human resources, marketing, and a multitude of safety, hygienic and employer compliance standards."

A Job, Career or Calling

Dr. Amy Wrzesniewski, an associate professor of organizational behaviour at Yale University, suggests that we can view our work as a job, a career, or a calling. According to Dr. Wrzesniewski, your work is a "job" if you are working primarily for the pay cheque. Whether it is earning money to pay the rent, support your children's education, or to fund your personal interests outside of work, your main orientation is financial. Rarely would you seek rewards that are not financial. This also means that you will change jobs frequently as you seek higher pay. Loyalty to your employer is low, except perhaps in one situation: where the financial reward in your current job is so high that other employers cannot, or will not, match it.

If you are primarily focused on moving up the corporate ladder, you likely view your work as a "career." In doing so, your main motivators are extrinsic. Receiving promotions, assuming new responsibilities, and gaining greater power and prestige are your driving forces. If this is your motivation, then titles, academic achievement, professional designations, recognition from others and an impressive resume mean a lot to you. But if job growth slows down, you will eventually become dissatisfied and likely seek work elsewhere.

Dr. Wrzesniewski says that if you love what you do and if you could afford it you would work for little or no pay, then your work is a "calling." For example, if you won the lottery and had complete financial independence, you would still continue to do this job. Here your motivators are intrinsic. You are passionate about what you do, see higher meaning in your work, and feel you are contributing to the greater good of society. There is almost no distinction between your day job and your personal life. The bottom line is that you're happier and more satisfied than most people, and will likely stay in that line of work for a long time.

Naturally, we might think that menial, repetitive work with low pay, no autonomy and little power would be considered a "job" while work that involves helping others, such as social work, health care or teaching, would be a "calling." But this is not the case.

Dr. Wrzesniewski discovered an interesting paradox. She found that those surveyed landed equally among the three orientations, regardless of occupation. So even among doctors, nurses, social workers and teachers, there are those doing their work just for the money. Likewise, there were postal carriers, hotel front desk clerks, labourers, and accounting clerks – all occupations that serve a very necessary function within organizations – who saw their work as a calling.

Passion Comes and Goes

Passion for work changes over time with more knowledge and experience. Let me give you an example.

Sophie, a recently-retired banker, told me that in her twenties she would have said her passion was sewing. "I would wear a different outfit every day for months – all clothing that I had made," she said.

Today she does not own a sewing machine and can barely stand to sew on a button. Had she followed her passion, she believes she would have ended up as a seamstress working for a low wage. Sophie got into banking because of a telephone call from a friend who convinced her to apply for a teller's job. She would never have considered applying for a job at a bank. But instead of just staying for a few years as she first thought, she ended up staying for 40.

As Sophie explained, it turned out she had a real talent for communication, sales, service and leadership. "I found out that my passion was learning and trying new things," she said. And she has certainly lived that passion. Starting with only a high school diploma, Sophie went on to obtain an undergraduate degree, MBA, and Chartered Financial Planner (CFP) designation – all funded by the bank – in addition to numerous other courses in coaching, mentorship and leadership. And during her career with the bank, she held 20 different positions including senior management roles domestically and internationally.

"Careers are a journey of discovery," she says. "The more open we are, the more we learn about ourselves and the opportunities available."

Anne-Marie, a professional accountant working for a membership association, provided sage advice when she told me her thoughts on the subject of passion for work:

> I am a pragmatist from a hardworking Dutch immigrant family and so my views are formative. Following one's passion in life or career is everyone's dream but in the end, we have to sustain ourselves and our families with good careers, long-term employability and, at the same time, contribute meaningfully to our communities.

> With that platform, we create a foundation from which pursuing our life's passion can ultimately be realized. This is when our passions and hobbies may turn into new careers. It's a longer-term view. Not many individuals have the financial means, support, or life circumstances – that foundation – to pursue their passions from the beginning. There are always those extraordinary exceptions of course.

> So, in my view, following one's passion may or may not be good advice, career or otherwise. But for most individuals taking a planned, responsible and reasoned approach with the right foundation will increase the likelihood of success. Our lives are long and we can achieve all of our goals, including our passions in life, by taking a longer-term view and never losing faith.

Tony, a medical physicist working at a cancer treatment centre, put it this way:

> The perfect combination is to have a career that is also your calling. It's hard not to be passionate about that.
>
> But in all honesty, I think most fortunate people find themselves in careers that facilitate the ability to meet their passions outside of their employment. Unfortunate people find themselves in jobs or careers that do not facilitate any degree of passion at or away from work. I'm fortunate to have a career with the work-life balance to engage with my passions outside of the work place. It's also much easier to remain passionate when I know the bills are getting paid.

So, is following your passion a good thing? My take on this topic is this: If you can find work that you're passionate about and make a decent living – go for it! That's the dream job.

But if you are like most people, try to find work that you *like* first, then master your trade. Like Sophie, your passion may grow in a totally different way than you might have first envisaged. And your perspective will change too.

For example, there are hair stylists who see their work as making people feel better about themselves – not just cutting or colouring hair. There are construction workers who see their work as creating affordable homes for young families to live in – not just laying bricks or hanging drywall. There are auto mechanics who see their work as ensuring cars operate reliably and safely – not just changing oil and checking the brakes.

The more successful you are at your trade, the more passionate you will be. As Scott Adams says, "We humans tend to enjoy things we're good at, while not enjoying things we suck at." That's typical Dilbert candour.

BEFORE MOVING ON

1. What do you think? Is following your passion good advice? What advice would you give to your children?

Chapter 2

What's Your Story?

**"We are products of our past
but we don't have to be prisoners of it."**

- Rick Warren, author, The Purpose Driven Life

UNDERSTANDING YOUR PAST is vital to moving ahead in your career. But getting to an understanding of who you really are and why you think and behave in certain ways is not as simple as it sounds. That's because most of us don't bother to take time to reflect on our lives. Or, if we do, we fool ourselves by only focusing on the good parts of the story – not on the failures and setbacks we may have experienced over the years.

Completing an honest self-reflection can enlighten you in many ways and lead to a better understanding of who you are and what you have to contribute. For example, by examining mistakes you've made in your life, you may be able to see patterns that have caused you pain or conflict over the years – whether in your personal life or at work. If you are willing to learn from your mistakes, you will avoid repeating these patterns.

In this chapter, I am going to ask you to craft your life story. Believe me, I get some weird looks when I ask my coaching clients to spend time on self-reflection in order to write their life story. Most people are uncomfortable doing something they may never have done. I explain that the process of self-reflection is important because you might discover things about yourself that have been hidden away for years, or discover why you behave the way you do. The only way to get at these explanations is to ask (and answer) the right questions.

This "writing your life story" exercise is all about understanding yourself and becoming more self-aware. While you cannot change your past, this process of self-discovery will make you more aware of how it affects your behaviour.

Let me give you an example illustrating the value of self-reflection.

Michael, a previous coaching client, had run a successful hair salon for years. By all external measures, Michael was successful. Financially, he was making enough money to maintain a comfortable life. Personally, he was married with a supportive wife and young daughter who attended private school. Professionally, his peers and customers held him in high regard and he had won several awards for his work. Michael was also healthy and fit and had completed three marathons over the previous two years. (His health was very important to him because he knew that serious health problems could seriously damage or even kill his business.)

Michael's business was thriving. In an industry where customers come and go, Michael had an exceptionally high retention rate – usually only losing customers when they moved away. Because of this, he saw no need to advertise. All new clients came from referrals, even though they sometimes had to wait several weeks or even months before getting a first appointment.

But despite Michael's outward success, he was dissatisfied. He regretted his long work hours and how his business was taking away from other aspects of his life, like family, running and golf. At a friend's suggestion, he had gone back to the previous years' calendar and discovered that he had only taken off 59 days in the entire year. This meant he was working on average six days a week, 52 weeks of the year.

While this hectic work schedule was financially rewarding, he was bothered by the potential impact on his long-term health and his family. More than anything, Michael knew that what created the busy work schedule was his own inability to say 'no' to customers. Michael told me that many times he would get calls from customers requesting an appointment for an "urgent" reason. Michael's typical response was something like, "Well, I finish at 7:00 tonight. Come on by then and I'll look after you."

It wasn't hard for Michael to see the conflict he was creating by this approach. On one hand, he had a satisfied customer and this pleased him very much. On the other hand, each time this happened he knew he was making a sacrifice from a family and personal perspective. Although he had been feeling this way for years, Michael resisted taking steps to correct the problem. And so his stress continued.

During our time together, Michael did a lot of self-reflection. I learned a number of details about his upbringing in a rural community and how his family struggled financially. His father, the main breadwinner in the house, worked in a trade where work was irregular. Although his father had a very strong work ethic, there just wasn't enough work around to keep him busy all the time. So he could never turn down work. If an employer called, his father always said yes. The time of day, day of the week or whatever else was going on didn't matter, when there was work to be had, Michael's father would go.

It didn't take Michael long to figure out this was the source of his problem. He recalled how he had always felt a surge of pride when he described his long work hours to his father – as if this was a badge of honour, something to be proud about. But the reality was that this behaviour – influenced by his father's behaviour – was affecting his life. He concluded this was something he had to change, even though it wouldn't be easy..

How to write your story

Here are a few suggestions on how to get the most out of this write-your-own-story exercise.

Find the right place and time to write. It is important that you get into the right mental state and environment to write. You should turn all your attention to the activity and find ways to avoid distraction such as television or kids. Also allow yourself enough time to complete the activity. You don't want to leave it half-finished or be rushed trying to complete it. Personally, I always find the best times to write are early mornings before everyone is up, or Saturday or Sunday afternoons, when there is less going on. I often choose my favourite coffee shop as a location to do this work, although a busy location like that might not work for you.

Write down your story to attain clarity. Writing your story is a much more effective process than simply thinking about it. The task of writing forces you to crystallize your thinking and go deeper into your topic. You are able to think through complex issues more clearly and precisely. For tasks that require deeper thought, I usually use pencil and paper. That may be old-school but for me it is more effective that typing on my laptop. If you don't like to write, you can always tape record your story.

Be brutally honest. When writing your story, there's no sense in fooling yourself by being less than 100 per cent honest.. Even if you don't like what you are uncovering, being honest with yourself is the only way to go.

Robert Steven Kaplan in his excellent book *What You're Really Meant To Do* points out that we all have competing narratives in own lives: a Success Narrative and a Failure Narrative. We can learn equally from both narratives.

Your Success Narrative is the one you tell most often, usually to impress people "in job interviews, when you meet new people, when you go on a date, when you talk to your children, and so forth." While this feels good, it is only half the story. That's because we also have a Failure Narrative, which rarely gets told. This narrative is about your self-doubts, worries, fears, and struggles we have that influence our actions and career decisions.

Because we tend to be embarrassed by our failure narrative, we usually overlook these important points. But as Kaplan points out, "The key is not to try to control or block out these thoughts. The point is to be aware of them … and, in particular, try to understand how they impact your decisions and behaviours."

Write your life story

Here is a list of questions you might consider to help you with your writing, although feel free to add important factors I may have omitted:

Where were you born? Describe your upbringing.
What were you parents like? What did they do? What beliefs did they hold?
Describe what your brothers and sisters were like.
Who were your best friends and how did they influence you?
What were your hobbies and interests?
What subjects interested you in school?
How did you do in school?
Who were your childhood heroes?
Who are – or were – your models? Why did you select them?
What are some highlights from your school years?
Why did you pursue your chosen courses of study in college or university?
What experiences in life have been most gratifying for you?
What experiences have been most difficult for you?
How have your early career jobs influenced who you are today?
What three people have had the greatest influence on your life and why?
Who were your best bosses and why?
Who were your worst bosses and why?
If you have children, how have they affected your outlook on life? How have your behaviours changed?
What jobs have been your best ones? What jobs have been your worst ones?
How well did you get along with your co-workers and bosses?
Are there any career moves you regretted?
Have you ever done something on the job that sabotaged your goals?
How have any volunteer or community activities affected your outlook on life or work?

When writing your story, remember that the purpose of this exercise is to learn about yourself so be specific: include the good and the bad, whether related to your upbringing, social life, friends, family, work, hobbies or school.

Bob's Story

Bob Shaw is a veteran sales and marketing executive who now serves others as regional director of a not-for-profit organization. Here is an excerpt from his life story.

Q. Who were your early influencers?
A. I am the son of a Royal Navy officer who immigrated to Canada in the late 1940s. His career had taken him around the world and that sense of adventure and intrigue about foreign cultures became part of our upbringing. We seldom sat at the kitchen table without an atlas or globe and Dad telling us where he had been. Those early years influenced my love for travel.

Tell us about your early career.
I started my career in the retail travel industry in the mid-1970s. It was an exciting time for me as the job enabled me to travel all over the world at someone else's expense. Frankly, I was more concerned with travelling to nice places than learning new skills, which was a mistake as I look back.

How did your career progress?
I eventually joined the Canadian Airlines/Air Atlantic team in a senior sales and marketing role. Here, I travelled from coast to coast which was hard on me and my personal life. I was a smoker and led a sedentary lifestyle. My first marriage broke up during this time. In my mid-30s, I started a travel industry marketing company and ultimately merged the firm into Carlson Wagonlit Travel. I stayed on as their director of marketing which necessitated a move to Toronto where I stayed for a number of years.

What has been your greatest learning?
In my early 40s, I got into the casino industry as VP Marketing with Caesars Gaming, a division of ITT Sheraton. I learned that while I had ambitions to go right to the top, I just did not have the capacity to do so. That was tough on my ego. You can develop skills but capacity is harder. We're not all wired the same to handle stress nor are we all

gifted with great abilities. Learning and accepting my own limitations was the greatest discovery for me up to that point in my career.

Was there a major turning point in your life?

In 2004, my second wife was diagnosed with Parkinson's disease. A year later, I had a heart attack. Around the same time, a business partnership I had went sour and ended up in court. All three events caused me to think deeper about what I should do with my life. Someone recommended I read *Encore* by Marc Freedman. When I did, it yelled at me: "This is you, Bob." That led me to find a new pathway to fulfillment.

What are you doing now?

I began volunteering with Parkinson's Society and realized how helping others made me feel good. Serendipitously, in 2012, the full-time position of Regional CEO of Parkinson's Society became available. I applied and was offered the job. This role has given me a real sense of purpose but more so gives me an emotional connection with my wife as she lives her life with Parkinson's. Every day I feel like I am doing something that inspires hope – not just in my wife's life but many others that I come in touch with daily.

BEFORE MOVING ON

1. Find the right location and sufficient time to sit down and write your life story. Be honest with yourself and do not avoid aspects of your life that make you feel uncomfortable.

2. When your life story is complete, take time to reflect on what you have written. What have you learned from the past? What have you learned about yourself? How has your story impacted your behaviours and values? How have your career choices been influenced by your story? What insights have you gleaned? How will your future behaviours change as a result of this story?

Chapter 3

Assessing Your
Skills and Abilities

**"Hard work spotlights the character of people:
some turn up their sleeves, some turn up their noses,
and some don't turn up at all."**

- Sam Ewing

THE WORDS "SKILLS" and "abilities" are often used interchangeably. For most people, *skills* are thought of as talents that are learned or acquired through training or actual hands-on experience. *Abilities,* on the other hand, are thought of as innate talents: things you do naturally, easily or effortlessly. For now, let's not worry about making a fine distinction between skills and abilities. Both are "must haves" for your career.

Most successful people – because their self-awareness is high – have a good understanding of their skills and abilities. While it may not come easily to them, they have learned that to succeed in their jobs and move ahead in their careers, they must be able to identify those qualities that allow them to improve.

Similarly, those who lack self-awareness often fail to grow and improve because they are unable to isolate what is holding them back. Once you have a firm grasp on your skills and abilities – and assuming you have the motivation to work on them – there is almost no limit to the progress you can make.

In this chapter, we are going to work through an exercise that will help you to better understand your own skills and abilities. In doing so, you will be able to also isolate your weaknesses. Then you can make a decision about whether or not to work on them.

Once you have a deeper understanding of your skills, abilities and weaknesses, you can decide how you want to apply this knowledge to your career strategy. As Robert Kaplan says in *What You're Really Meant To Do*, the key questions you should ask yourself are:

> Should you focus more on your strengths?
> Should you seek jobs that play to your strengths or jobs that help you improve in areas where you are weak?
> Do you need to be good at everything?
> Should you avoid jobs where your weaknesses might materially undermine your performance?

All good questions to think about after you have completed your evaluation. Remember – understanding your own skills and abilities is *your* responsibility. Yes, you may seek the input and feedback of bosses, colleagues, coaches, and friends but ownership of the on-going exercise rests with you.

Let's do the exercise.

On the following pages, you will find a list of over 100 skills and abilities. You might think of some as "personal" such as *patience*. Others might be considered "functional" like *auditing financial data*. While this is a long list, it may not be absolutely comprehensive. So, go ahead and add others to the list as you wish.

Your task is to rate yourself on each skill. Don't limit yourself to a certain number – feel free to check as many as you like. You can use a rating system of:

- Skill is well-developed (+)
- Skill is under-developed (-)
- Not sure (NS), or
- Not relevant (NR) if you will never use this skill anywhere.

Skills and Abilities

Accuracy
Adaptability
Administering
Advising people
Analytical skills
Assembling equipment
Attention to detail
Auditing financial data
Being thorough
Brainstorming
Budgeting
Building new business
Business management skills
Calculating data
Categorizing records
Checking for accuracy
Coaching skills
Collaborating ideas
Collecting items
Communication skills
Conflict resolution
Constructing things
Counseling people
Creative thinking skills
Critical thinking skills
Customer service skills
Decision making skills
Defining problems
Delegating
Designing systems
Determination
Developing plans
Diplomacy
Editing
Encouraging others
Enforcing rules
Entertaining others
Envisioning solutions
Estimating
Expressing feelings

Expressing ideas
Extracting information
Focusing
Gathering information
Generating business
Goal setting
Initiating projects
Handling money
Information management
Inspecting things
Interacting with people
Interviewing
Inventing products/ideas
Investigating solutions
Knowledge of community
Knowledge of concepts
Leading teams
Listening to people
Maintaining focus
Maintaining schedules or times
Managing organizations
Managing people
Mediating between people
Meeting deadlines
Meeting new people
Motivating others
Multi-tasking
Navigating politics
Negotiating
Operating equipment
Organizing
Patience
People management skills
Performing clerical duties
Performing numerical analysis
Persuading others
Planning meetings
Planning
Predicting future trends
Problem solving

Product promotion	Selling products or services
Productivity	Serving people
Proposing ideas	Setting performance standards
Providing discipline	Sketching charts or diagrams
Public speaking	Strategic thinking
Questioning others	Stress management
Raising funds	Summarizing data
Reading	Supervising employees
Recognizing problems	Supporting others
Recruiting	Taking decisive action
Rehabilitating people	Taking initiative
Relating to others	Teaching others
Reliability	Team building
Repairing equipment	Teamwork skills
Reporting data	Technical work
Researching	Thinking logically
Resolving conflicts	Time management skills
Resourcefulness	Training skills
Responsibility	Translating words
Results oriented	Using computers
Risk taking	Verbal communication skills
Running meetings	Working creatively
Scheduling	Working under pressure
Self-motivated	Working with statistics
Selling ideas	Writing clearly and concisely

Once you have completed the exercise, take some time and think about it. Then, list the top eight skills and abilities that describe you the best:

1.

2.

3.

4.

5.

6.

7.

8.

BEFORE MOVING ON

1. Ensure you complete the exercise to determine your top eight skills and abilities. Seek feedback from others to gain their honest perspective on your list but don't forget: you "own" the list.

2. Once you have arrived at a final list, answer these questions from Robert Kaplan's book *What You're Really Meant To Do*: Should you focus more on these strengths? Should you seek jobs that play to your strengths? Or, jobs that help you improve in areas where you are weak? Do you need to be good at everything? Should you avoid jobs where your weaknesses might materially undermine your performance?

3. Think about how you would describe your skills in a job interview. (A common interview questions is: Tell me your top three skills and how you applied those skills in your previous job.)

4. While you're at it, think about how you would answer the "Tell me your top three weaknesses" question in an interview. Remember: you shouldn't be embarrassed to admit your weaknesses. However, you should either be working on fixing them (if they are important to your career direction) or delegating them to others who are better at them than you. For example, if you want to be an accountant but your attention to detail is bad, that's a problem. You better fix it. But if your mechanical abilities are lacking, that's not a problem if you have no desire to become a mechanic. You can always hire somebody to fix your car.

Chapter 4

You'll Be Happier If Your Work and Values Align

"Generally the things we value the most … in our 20s, 30s and 40s become the things we value the least at the end of our lives. And all those things that so many value least, like deep human connections, random acts of kindness, being in superb physical condition, devoting ourselves to excellence in our work, creating a legacy and carving out time each day to work on ourselves …. will in the end reveal themselves to be most valuable."

- Robin Sharma, *Discover Your Destiny*

AFTER MANY YEARS of coaching people, I've concluded that the greatest cause of career unhappiness is when people are forced to work in conflict with their values.

Interestingly, a large number of these same people incorrectly diagnose the cause of this unhappiness. They come to me believing that more money or vacation, flexible work hours, a job closer to home, or even a new boss, will cure their unhappiness. Yet when these changes do occur, more often than not, their unhappiness remains.

Why does this misdiagnosis occur? Why can't people see something that should be obvious? It's embarrassing to admit but the reality is that most of us feel too busy to search for the real meaning of our lives – what we believe in and want from our lives. Plus, it's hard work. Coming to a deep understanding of our values takes effort. So too often, we avoid it.

But the result is that in the absence of a sense of purpose, we inadvertently let others make our decisions and tell us what things mean, until we reach a breaking point and can't go any further.

Let me give you a couple of examples. I met with David to discuss a career dilemma he was facing. When we met, David was a 45-year old, senior manager with a major financial services company. He had impressive credentials, a solid track record of accomplishments, and above-average compensation, which allowed him to enjoy the finer things in life. He also had a very promising future with his company. The problem was: he was beginning to resent his work and his employer and was not sure he wanted to do that job for the rest of his career.

I learned that David's job had evolved into two broad functions: dealing with staff issues (problems, he calls them) and head office reporting, which he said had become highly politicized. The enjoyment he once felt from his work was gone. Personally, he'd rather spend more time "in the field" with his customers – the lifeblood of the business.

The demands of his work also were having a big impact on David's personal life. He told me that he'd much rather spend more time with his teenage son, fishing and camping which they both love, and focusing on a more regular exercise routine. Instead, he has been toiling away at the office for 12 to 14 hours a day, a pace he realized must be kept up occasionally, but not all the time. The problem was there was no end in sight: this work schedule was unlikely to lessen any time soon.

So while David had all the appearances of success – a good income, fancy title, comfortable work surroundings and prestigious employer – deep down, he was unhappy. And the source of that unhappiness was the gap between his behaviours and his values. None of the things he valued most – balance in life, nature, a regular exercise program, and time with family – were being met, because of his work.

In our conversations, and through coaching, I encouraged David to consider self-employment in his own field. While there are clear risks involved, mainly financial, I believe that option is attainable and it should allow him to live closer to his true values. As I write this, David is reviewing this option, including finding ways to mitigate the financial risk.

Understanding what's important

Let me give you an example of another client who based his own career selection on his personal values. Several years ago, I met Chris, then a 32-year old recent MBA graduate. Originally from Montreal, Chris had about five years' sales and marketing experience with a mid-sized communications agency in that city. Chris also possessed a true passion for the outdoors. A few years prior, he had successfully completed an outdoor leadership training program and since then had led several wilderness adventure excursions in the Canadian Rockies and throughout the interior of British Columbia.

Chris had decided to leave Montreal to complete his MBA and selected a well-known program in a smaller city. He enjoyed his two years away from Montreal very much, particularly since it afforded him the opportunity to enjoy the outdoors. Now that Chris had graduated, he felt he "had to get on with his life." The question was what should he do?

Like most MBA graduates, Chris felt the pull toward a career with a large corporation. Big jobs, important sounding titles and attractive compensation, in his view, seemed to be the primary motivators for many of his fellow graduates. Plus, MBA programs appeared to encourage students in that direction as little time and course content was directed toward small business or the not-for-profit sector.

As Chris graduated and many of the classmates with whom he had shared great times over the previous two years, moved away to launch their careers, Chris found himself in a dilemma. Intuitively, he did not feel that working in a large corporate environment was the right thing for him: "The thought of sitting in a cubicle in a tall building somewhere pushing paper, does not turn me on," he says. Plus he had grown to like the smaller city he was now living in. Two of his sisters and their families had relocated there recently and it was starting to feel like home although his best friends all still lived in Montreal.

As Chris analyzed his various career options, one variable that he used subconsciously when assessing each option was, "What would my friends and family think?" He worried for example that if he worked in a not-for-profit organization that his fellow classmates would question his judgment. He worried that if he took a job that didn't pay well, regardless of how enjoyable the job might be, his parents would be disappointed. He worried that if he remained in the small city, where he now lived, that his friends in Montreal might suggest his MBA was a waste.

Mind you, not one of his family, friends or classmates had even remotely suggested any of these things. Yet Chris was constantly analyzing his career options through the framework of what others would think. He was deciding his future, not based on his own values and wishes, but through the lenses of others.

Thankfully, after several months of reflection, Chris came to the realization that he must make his career decisions based on what he was passionate about, what he truly valued, not what others think. Like many others before him, he could have chosen a career path that pleased his parents. He could have taken a corporate job like many of his friends and classmates. Or, he might even have ended up in a job simply because it was a "job" – one that paid the bills. But he was determined that he could not and would not live his life based on the expectations of others. Separating these variables was not going to be easy, but he was determined to do it.

Chris has since landed in a very rewarding job: working in a marketing capacity for a company that is providing services to elite athletes. He is doing exciting work in a location and physical environment that he loves and has a very promising future ahead of him. Chris could easily have ended up in a career "by accident." Thankfully he came to the realization that he must act according to his own values before it was too late.

Identifying your deeply-held values

Chris did what everyone should do. He let his values guide his actions and shape his career path.

Now it's your turn. Here is an exercise that will help you identify values that are most important to you. Remember, they are a product of many things in your life: your upbringing, your parents, your education, your spiritual upbringing, your teachers and mentors, your early bosses, and so on. And there are no right or wrong answers. They are unique to you.

Read through the list of values on the next page and rate the degree of importance you would assign to each one using the following scale:

5 – Critically important *(Guides all of my actions and behaviours)*
4 – Very important *(Pretty significant motivator in my life)*
3 – Reasonably important *(Am occasionally influenced by this value)*
2 – Somewhat important *(Give it a little thought but not much more)*
1 – Not important *(Does not motivate me)*

Feel free to add any other values, not on the list, that are important to you.

Values List

Achievement	Empathy	Leadership
Adventure	Ethics	Learning
Affiliation	Fairness	Loyalty
Ambition	Family	Moral fulfillment
Authenticity	Fast-paced	Openness
Autonomy	Flexibility	Order
Balance	Friendship	Originality
Beauty	Fun	Perfection
Belonging	Generosity	Perseverance
Challenge	Growth	Power
Change	Happiness	Recognition
Commitment	Harmony	Respect
Community	Health	Responsibility
Compassion	Helping	Security
Competition	Honesty	Service to others
Conformity	Humility	Simplicity
Control	Humour	Spirituality
Courage	Independence	Spontaneity
Creativity	Influence	Stability
Decisiveness	Insight	Status
Discipline	Intellectual	Teamwork
Diversity	Integrity	Tradition
Economic reward	Kindness	Winning
Environment	Knowledge	Wisdom

Turning values into action

By itself, a value is meaningless if it fails to motivate you to action. To be meaningful, a value must influence the choices you make daily. Saying you have certain values but behaving in a manner that is inconsistent with those statements is deceitful and indicates a serious disconnect between your inner thoughts and outward behaviours.

Think about the ratings you gave. Which ones resonate most strongly? Now, select your _five_ most important values and answer three questions:

- Why is this value important to you?
- To what degree is this value being met through your work or career choices?
- Are there times when my work was in conflict with this value?

Value #1: _____

Value #2: _____

Value #3: _____

Value #4: _____

Value #5: _____

Your personal vision statement

As Jim Loehr and Tony Schwartz, authors of *The Power of Full Engagement* write, "The issue is not so much whether your life is providing you with a sense of meaning. The issue is whether you are actively using life as a vehicle through which to express your deepest values."

I encourage you to take this exercise even one step further and create a personal vision statement that reflects your values and at the same time presents a framework for how to plan to invest your time and energy.

A vision statement should strike a balance. On one hand, it should be high-level, expressing those intrinsic, deeply held beliefs that govern all aspects of your life. On the other hand, the statement should be practical and realistic. If it achieves this level of practicality and realism, it can be used continually as a blueprint against which to evaluate all major decisions in your career and your life. It will allow you to act in ways that are consistent with your values and turn aside with conviction those career opportunities that conflict.

Some individuals write both a personal vision statement and a professional vision statement. Some choose to create a single document that encompasses both personal and professional. The format is your choice. Just write whatever feels best for you. You will have ample opportunity to re-write and edit your document before settling on a final version.

For your reference, here are three sample vision statements, prepared by other individuals.

Sample Vision Statement #1

> I value myself as an individual and strive to have balance in my life. This balance will allow me to support all other values that I have. My family and friends are key parts of my life that keep me focused on what the true meaning of life is.

> It is important to me to have open, honest relationships with all people in my life. It is important for me to be generous and thoughtful and remember that life is bigger than just me.

> I want to continue learning about myself and pushing my growth so that I can be the best person that I can be and help others to realize their own gifts. I enjoy being independent and will strive for

excellence in everything that I do. My health is a priority. I want to have fun on the journey.

Sample Vision Statement #2

I will:
- Live a healthy, active lifestyle.
- Engage in meaningful and enjoyable work that helps other people learn and grow.
- Be community-minded, sharing my time and talents with those people and organizations who need them.
- Maintain a positive perspective on life, always looking for the good in people and events.
- Pro-actively nurture relationships with existing and new friends.
- Act in a financially responsible manner, living within my means and planning for the future.
- Continue to learn new things, be open to and explore new ideas and different ways of doing things.
- Live a simpler lifestyle – spend less time working and more time developing outside interests.
- Maintain relationships that are open, communicative, respectful and non-judgmental.

Sample Vision Statement #3

Personally, in my final chapter, I only hope to enjoy looking at myself in the mirror as much as when I was a young boy. That is to say with no regrets and knowing that I gave it my all and was part of the larger good.

The path I have chosen is one dictated primarily by passion, integrity, commitment and respect. Key for me is learning from others while at the same time, sharing my experiences. Every decision we make has implications so choices such as healthy life style and strong family relationships are key.

My daily goal is to learn, to contribute and to have fun. Maintaining a sense of humour is key while staying focused on the positive and not making negative assumptions (often incorrect) or unfairly judging others.

Possessions are not how I want to be judged but rather by the respect of my family, friends and colleagues and others who have come to know me.

BEFORE MOVING ON

1. Think about your top 5 values list – the values that should guide almost everything you do. How have these values shaped your career direction to date?

2. Prepare a vision statement that encompasses both your personal and professional life. Put this statement in a prominent location where you can review it frequently. You might also want to review it with family and friends to see if they see you in the same light.

Chapter 5

Learn From Previous Jobs

**"If you are unwilling to learn, no one can help you.
If you are determined to learn, no one can stop you."**

- Unknown

ONE OF THE best things you can do to avoid repeating your career mistakes and move toward a job that fits well is to analyze all your past jobs to identify the aspects of those jobs that you enjoyed and did not enjoy.

If this is done well, what you will discover is that there are common threads among your various jobs. You will discover that what you liked about one job tended to be the same through all your jobs. Similarly, what you disliked will likely be the same through all your jobs.

Take Colin, for example, who came from a family of bankers. From a young age, Colin was groomed to go into banking. While in university, all his work terms were with banks and everyone in his family thought that banking was a "good, stable job" especially if he ever planned to have a family of his own. So Colin did what the family expected – upon graduation, he joined a bank.

But after a few months on the job, he found he wasn't enjoying it. "Just give it more time," he told himself, thinking he would eventually get used to it. But that never happened. In looking at his job seriously, he discovered that he disliked the structure and formality of the bank and he didn't like the actual work.

What he did like was dealing with people and that led him to quit the bank and return to school to complete his MBA in human resources. Today, he is a senior human resources manager with a large NGO. His advice: "If it isn't working, stop and think. Talk to others outside your network and find people who can help you see it objectively."

Let's do an exercise to help you isolate the things you liked and didn't like about past jobs. In the table below, list all the significant jobs you've held starting with the oldest. You should include all jobs whether summer or seasonal, part-time, contract, or full-time. You should also include all significant volunteer opportunities as these roles can also give you a good sense of what it's like to work in those organizations.

For each role, think about pay, people you worked with, job duties, hours of work, work culture, and anything else that could influence your satisfaction levels. Then, apply this rating system to each one:

1 – Absolutely hated this job
2 – Generally did *not* like going to work
3 – Happy some days; not so happy other days
4 – Enjoyed going to work most days
5 – Absolutely loved this job

Job   **Rating**

1.

2.

3.

4.

5.

6.

7.

8.

Let's look at each job in detail and what you enjoyed and did not enjoy about each one.

What I enjoyed   **What I did not enjoy**

Job 1

_____

_____

_____

Job 2

_____

_____

_____

Job 3

_____

_____

_____

Job 4

_____

_____

_____

Job 5

_____

_____

_____

Job 6

_____

_____

_____

Job 7

_____

_____

_____

Job 8

_____

_____

_____

BEFORE MOVING ON

1. Sit back and review your list of what you enjoyed and did not enjoy. What are the common threads? When have you enjoyed your work the most? When have you enjoyed your work the least?

Sarah's Story

After having two children, **Sarah Williams** decided to set aside the rigour and pressures of corporate life and now operates two home-based businesses.

Q: Tell us your early background.
A: Despite coming from an entrepreneurial family, I took a marketing job with a major corporation after finishing my MBA. I stayed there almost ten years during which time I took two one-year maternity leaves. During my second maternity leave, I started doing some entrepreneurial things, like making and selling children's cakes to other parents. That gave me a bit of a taste for a different life. When I returned to work after the leave, I managed to negotiate a four-day work week. This not only meant I could spend more time with the kids but it allowed me some freedom to continue with the cake business.

Then what happened?
Not long after, my husband, who ran his own consulting business, suggested I might want to consider quitting my job and focus on working from home. At that time, we owned a "hobby" company that

we worked on from 8:00 pm to midnight and thought we might be able to expand it. After seriously considering the financial risks associated with such a move, I decided to take the plunge and quit my job.

Did you have any doubt about leaving corporate life at the time?
Yes, absolutely. I left my employer in May and had planned to take the summer off and spend time with the kids. Reality did not hit until September, when I had to figure out how to make money. To tell the truth, it took a lot longer than I expected to get going and make any reasonable level of income.

How have your businesses evolved?
We had been making some money all along through our "hobby" company, Urban Parent, which is an online resource for local parents. We publish an events calendar and a daily blog. Revenue comes through advertising from local organizations who want to promote their activities. We now have sites in two cities and plan to expand to other cities across Canada.

Then I started another company called "Gluestix" that makes simple craft kits for parents to use with their children. I started out doing craft shows and revenue started to flow in right away. But my big break was when a company in Calgary that runs a kids party for the stampede, ordered 80 kits. Now I have lots of customers in Calgary.

How is being an entrepreneur different from corporate life?
In the beginning, I ended up wasting a lot of time because I didn't have the discipline of going to work at a set time every day. So, instead of getting out there and figuring out how I was going to make this work, I'd end up going to the gym or for coffee with a friend. I've since learned how to build structure into my schedule even though I don't have to report to anybody. It can also be lonely being on your own, especially when you work from home.

Do you ever envisage returning to corporate life?
From time to time I do get tempted by really cool jobs with interesting companies, but when I think about it seriously, I also say "no." I can say for sure that I am never tempted by corporate jobs where you'd have to sit in a cubicle all day. I know, with absolute certainty, that I don't want to ever go into cubicle life again.

Chapter 6

Translate Your Interests
Into Career Options

**"It's all in your mind. Whatever you hold in your mind will tend to occur in
your life. If you continue to believe as you have always believed,
you will continue to act as you have always acted."**

- Anonymous

PSYCHOLOGIST JOHN HOLLAND (1919-2008) pioneered one of the most
commonly-used frameworks, now called the Holland Code, to help people
understand the relationship between personality and interests and their career
choices. In his work, Holland concluded that people are more likely to excel and
experience job satisfaction if they are able to express their personalities through
their work.

For example, if you are friendly, outgoing and like helping other people, you
might find careers such as teaching, nursing and social work more satisfying
than ones which involve working by yourself in an office cubicle. Likewise, if
you are a practical, get-things-done sort of person, you may become frustrated
working in an environment where everyone else prefers to sit back and discuss
abstract ideas.

While this may seem obvious as you read it, it is surprising how many people
get it mixed up and end up in jobs that do not match their personality.

Holland's model used six groupings to help people identify their personality
preferences:

Realistic (aka "doers") people tend to excel in jobs that produce tangible results.
Not surprisingly, they are mechanically inclined and enjoy working with tools
and machines while they fix, build and repair things. The jobs that satisfy them

the most usually involve physical activity and are very much hands-on. For the most part, these people would rather avoid dealing with people and discussing abstract ideas. They also avoid reams of data and just want to get down to solving problems. They also tend to avoid careers that involve dealing with others – like social work or counselling – and instead are drawn to careers that require problem solving like computer technician, architect, electrician and plumber.

Investigative (aka "thinkers") people prefer thinking over doing. They are most satisfied when their work involves tasks such as developing ideas, conducting research, gathering information, and analyzing trends and figuring out what they mean. The more complex the problem is, the happier they are. Since they are at their best sorting through problems on their own, they usually avoid working in large teams.

Artistic (aka "creators") people are creative, sensitive, innovative and non-conforming. Like Investigative types, they prefer to work with ideas and concepts but tend to express themselves – not in science or technology – but in art, writing, dance, theatre, or design. They do their best work in unstructured environments that offer a lot of variety and change and will avoid occupations that are too conventional or traditional.

Social (aka "helpers") individuals like to work with people. By nature, they are caring, helpful and friendly. They prefer doing work that involves social interaction and helping others. They like working in teams and are very effective solving problems collaboratively. Since their focus is "people", they do not like a lot of numbers or data and they avoid physical work that might require that they use machines or tools. You will see social people drawn to careers in nursing, teaching, counselling, and other occupations that involve helping people.

Enterprising (aka "persuaders") people prefer to lead and influence others to achieve business or organizational goals. Because they are usually extroverted, ambitious, and confident, they thrive in work environments where they are in charge. In these roles, they often achieve status and recognition – something they value very much. And because they are so persuasive and motivational, they are effective in getting other people to "jump on board." Not surprisingly, careers like law, business, and entrepreneurship are ones that fit this interest most.

Conventional (aka "organizers") people value precision, accuracy and clearly-defined procedures. They are at their best when organizing activities that require a lot of attention to detail and planning. They approach work methodically and are conscientious and efficient in getting things done. Generally, they work better in structured environments, like large organizations, and lean toward careers in accounting, engineering, human resources and administration.

Where do your interests lie?

Here is a small exercise called an interests inventory that will help you identify your own interests clearly and relate them to various career options. Unfortunately this exercise will not tell you *exactly* what job is best for you – if only it were that easy. But it will at least stimulate your thinking about what areas *appear* to fit your interests and hold the best promise for a rewarding career.

For each statement listed, insert the number that most closely reflects how you feel using this scale:

4 – I *strongly agree* with this statement
3 – I *somewhat agree* with this statement
2 – I *somewhat disagree* with this statement
1 – I *strongly disagree* with this statement

Realistic interests	**(1-4)**
I like to work with my hands	_____
I like to repair things	_____
I like to work with tools	_____
I like to operate machinery	_____
I like physical work	_____
I like to work outdoors	_____
Total score	_____

Investigative interests	**(1-4)**
I like to solve puzzles	_____
I like ambiguous challenges	_____
I like to read and study	_____
I like math and science	_____
I like to investigate physical things	_____
I like to discuss problems	_____
Total score	_____

Artistic interests   **(1-4)**

I like to express myself   _____

I like freedom from structure   _____

I like unconventional solutions   _____

I like to express myself visually   _____

I like to work alone   _____

I like opportunities to be creative   _____

Total score   ========

Social interests   **(1-4)**

I like to care for others   _____

I like to work with people   _____

I like to be part of a group   _____

I like to train others   _____

I like to supervise people   _____

I like to help others   _____

Total score   ========

Enterprising interests   **(1-4)**

I like to persuade others   _____

I like to be the leader   _____

I like to speak to groups   _____

I like to manage projects   _____

I like to sell things   _____

I like to make things happen   _____

Total score   ========

Conventional interests   **(1-4)**

I like things to be orderly   _____

I like well-defined tasks   _____

I like following office procedures   _____

I like stable situations   _____

I like having a chain of command   _____

I like to know what is coming next   _____

Total score   ========

Now record your total score for each category (from highest to lowest) to see where your greatest interests lie and then take a look at possible careers (on the following two pages) that match those interests. As Holland and others point out, don't limit your search to careers that fall only under your highest interest. You should consider those within your top three interests.

Interest	My Score
1	
2.	
3.	
4.	
5.	

Possible career options

Realistic	Investigative	Artistic
agriculture	actuary	advertising
architect	biologist	architect
carpenter	chemist	art teacher
CAD designer	chiropractor	author/writer
chef	college professor	broadcaster
chemist	computer programmer	chef
computer technician	dental hygienist	commercial artist
dentist	dietician	copy writer
electrician	electronic technician	dance instructor
engineer	engineer	fashion designer
firefighter	geologist	fine artist
graphic designer	lawyer	interior decorator
musician	medical technician	journalist
painter	mathematician	language teacher
photographer	physiotherapist	librarian
physiotherapist	science instructor	musician
plumber	pharmacology	photographer
police officer	physician	PR specialist
printer	psychologist	web designer
sheet metal worker	surveyor	writer
tool and die maker	systems analyst	

Social	Enterprising	Conventional
athletic trainer	business owner	accountant
child care worker	buyer	actuary
clergy	caterer	administrator
cosmetologist	chef	archivist
counsellor	consultant	auditor
customer service rep	entrepreneur	banker
dental hygienist	fundraiser	bookkeeper
dietician	graphic designer	carpenter
elementary teacher	hotel manager	chemist
fitness trainer	HR manager	court reporter
guidance counselor	journalist	credit manager
human resources	lawyer	customer service
nurse	manufacturing rep	dietician
non-profit director	market researcher	economist
social worker	marketing specialist	engineer
special ed. teacher	merchandiser	finance
therapist	public relations	food service
veterinarian	real estate agent	human resources
	sales person	medical assistant
	school administrator	pharmacist
	travel agent	tax professional
		teacher
		technical writer

BEFORE MOVING ON

1. Think about some of the career options this exercise has suggested might fit your interests. Are these jobs you could see yourself doing? Do you have the necessary training and skills to consider them? How might you explore these options further?

Chapter 7

What Do You Want
From Your Work?

"Find a job you like and you add five days to every week."

- H. Jackson Brown, Jr.

HERE IS WHERE you are going to imagine the characteristics of your ideal job and determine which ones are absolutely essential to you as you move ahead in your career. Let's start right now by writing down your career needs in each area. If something doesn't matter to you, just write "Does not matter." Or, if you want to add something that is not already on the list, go ahead and add it.

Compensation. How much do you *want* to make in your next job? How much do you *need* to make in your next job? Are you comfortable with a form of incentive-based pay? Note: It's important for you to set your bottom line, the salary that you cannot go below to meet your needs.

Job security. How important is job security to you?

Benefits. What benefit coverage do you need? Are there other benefits, such as flex-time or a shorter work day, that you would accept if your salary target is not met? Might you be able to purchase certain benefits on your own if your employer doesn't provide them?

Vacation. How much vacation do you want given your years of work?

Physical location. Where do you want to work? How far away is it from your home? How would you plan to get to work: car, bike, walk, transit? Is it in an urban, suburban or rural area? What amenities are nearby?

Workspace. What would you like your workspace to be like: open workspace, private office, natural light, etc.? Would you prefer to work from a home office? Describe the overall physical work environment that you prefer.

Industry. What industry sectors appeal to you? Which ones match your values?

Company. Would you prefer to work with a small start-up, or a growing entrepreneurial company, or a large well-established organization? Does company size matter? How important is the company's reputation and why? Is it important that the company be socially responsible?

Good boss. What kind of boss would you like to work for? Would you like them to be hands-on, giving you lots of direction, or do you prefer more autonomy? What leadership qualities does your ideal boss have?

People. What types of people do you like to work with? (co-workers, customers, employees). Do you prefer to work with a large or small number of people? Do you prefer to work on your own?

Status and title. Answer honestly: how important is status and title to you? Do you want these to reflect your relative rank?

Personal and professional growth. What are your expectations around growth? Do you need to work for an employer who encourages and offers professional development and lots of opportunity to learn new things?

Type of work. What type of work would you prefer to do? Should your work be meaningful – such as helping others versus making money for your employer? What scope of responsibility do you prefer? Describe the level of challenge you need.

Opportunity for advancement. What types of advancement opportunities (upward; lateral; new location) are you seeking?

Recognition. To what degree do you need to be recognized and acknowledged for your work?

Culture. How important is the company's reputation to you and why? Is it important that the company be socially responsible? Should they have a clear sense of mission, values and goals?

BEFORE MOVING ON

1. What you've defined above is your "ideal job." We all know that it is impossible to achieve everything on that list. You will have to make choices. Take a look at the list again. Which ones are most important to you? Try to group them into three categories:

    Category A: Absolutely essential that you have these in a job;
    Category B: Very important to you but not *absolutely* essential;
    Category C: Of lesser importance, but still nice to have

Chapter 8

Pulling It All Together

**"If you take too long in deciding what to do with your life,
you'll find you've done it."**

- Pam Shaw

NOW IS THE time to pull together everything from this section. Take a look over all the exercises you've completed: interests, skills, values, career needs, life story and things you enjoyed (and didn't) from past jobs.

Are there any patterns or themes that are emerging? Are you having any gut reactions, good or bad, to what you've been asked to consider? Are there any career options you know you want to avoid?

Remember: the goal of this entire section is to bring clarity to your job search. Doing so will lead to a more organized and focused job search campaign so you will not waste your time targeting roles that do not match your strengths or interests. Instead, you'll be able to quickly size up an opportunity and determine if it is the right fit for you.

Likewise, you will be better prepared to answer interview questions about your skills, strengths, weaknesses and accomplishments. Most employers look for and appreciate candidates who can accurately describe themselves, even if they're describing a weakness. You will come across as reflective and self-aware; two qualities that will help you get jobs and grow your career.

Start writing down the definition of the role you are seeking. When doing so, try to be as specific as possible. After you are satisfied with your own response, start testing it with friends and colleagues. Ask them to give you constructive feedback. Does it make sense? Does it sound like you?

The type of job I am seeking is:

_____

_____

_____

_____

_____

_____

_____

_____

_____

_____

_____

_____

_____

And remember, this still is – and always will be – a work in progress. As you start your search and meet with more and more people, you will refine the ideas you have developed in this chapter. You will drop some and come up with new ones. You will find some of the paths you thought were open are in fact closed. Often, new ones will open up, often they are pathways you hadn't even contemplated before. Even though you have a "plan", be open to new ideas, thoughts and perspectives.

As Marci Alboher says in *The Encore Career Handbook*, "You may go down several paths before you determine what you want to do. And going down a path … can be a detour that lasts months or even years. But don't equate a detour with a waste of time. You are on a journey. If you learn that a certain kind of work isn't what you want, that's progress. When you are on a journey, expect some discoveries that take you in an entirely unexpected direction."

Ask Gerry

Q. How do I know when the time is right to start looking for a new job?

A. Making the decision to look for another job can be disruptive to your career, reputation and personal life. You may lose relationships and income and blemish your resume if you move to the wrong job. But staying in your present job – because you fear the uncertainty of a move – can be worse. You can become stagnant and reduce your chances of finding a job later on.

Take a look at your employer first. There may be no future for you if:

- You're not being invited to participate in meetings.
- You are being undervalued and disrespected.
- Your compensation is less than others in similar positions.
- You have frequent disagreements with your boss.
- There is no recognition or thanks for your work.
- Your colleagues don't associate or consult with you.
- You are being given work that is beneath your abilities.

Even if none of these things exist and your employer is happy with your work, you might consider a change if:

- There is no obvious role for you to grow into.
- You have maxed-out your learning in your current job.
- You have lost your enthusiasm for your job.
- There is a gap between your values and those of senior management.
- Your boss changes and she does not appreciate your contribution.
- Your job is so stressful that it is taking a toll on your health and family.

Some people start looking for another job if they've had a bad day or a clash with their boss. Be careful of these situations. Ask yourself if this is a one-time occurrence or is it evidence of a genuine mismatch that is unlikely to change?

Section Two

The Toolbox

**"On your resume, in your cover letters and in your interviews …
convey your passion and link your strengths to measurable results.
Employers and interviewers love concrete data."**

- Marcus Buckingham

Chapter 9

How to Build an Extraordinary Resume

"Resume: a written exaggeration of only the good things a person has done in the past, as well as a wish list of the qualities a person would like to have."

- Bo Bennett, *author, Year to Success*

CONSIDER THESE ODDS. Most employers will receive more than 100 resumes for a single job opening. These same employers then spend just 20 – 30 seconds reading each resume. They then select between 10% and 20% of applicants for interviews.

This means the odds of you being selected for an interview are low – even if you are a great candidate. In fact, I believe that in many cases the best candidate doesn't get selected for an interview because they haven't presented their resume in a way that makes their qualifications and experience stand out. Don't make the reader work too hard to figure out your background. You can make their life easier by presenting your background in a clear, easy-to-read layout.

There are two forms of resumes: chronological and functional. Let's start with the chronological resume, which is the most commonly-used form of resume and the format most preferred by recruiters and employers. As the name implies, a chronological resume lists your work experience in chronological order with the current (or most recent) position being listed first.

The reason why employers prefer this format is that it presents your work history in the most logical sequence of events. It shows your advancement from one position to another and tracks your career progress overall. It immediately identifies gaps in your work history and other unusual occurrences. It isn't that these are bad things. But employers will want to get a bit more information on anything that stands out.

Here is the normal flow of a chronological resume starting from the top:

Heading

Your name should be shown in the way you prefer to be called. While your formal name might be Thomas Jones but you prefer just 'Tom', then show your name as Thomas (Tom) Jones or simply Tom Jones. Do not include your middle initial as this has gone out of style.

You no longer have to include your civic address at the top of resume. It is unlikely any employer is going to be sending you anything by mail plus it could introduce the risk of economic profiling or an incorrect conclusion about length of your commute.

Just put your preferred email address and phone number where you can be reached most easily. If you have a social media presence, (which you should after reading this book) include those links especially your LinkedIn profile and Twitter handle.

There is one exception where it may be to your benefit to include your civic address: If you are moving from one part of the country to another part and you want to show you have a residence in your new location as you apply for jobs. In that instance, it makes sense to have a local address to convey to the employer that you are available to meet them in person and on short notice. This is an especially helpful strategy if your cell phone number still has your old area code.

By the way, if you list addresses, use the Canada Post version of postal codes, two letters without periods, e.g. BC for British Columbia, AB for Alberta, and so on.

Some people list their degrees and designations behind their names in the header. Others choose not to because there is usually an entire Education section on your resume. I will leave that choice to you. If you do decide to include these achievements, you should limit them to two only. These should be from degree granting institutions (or community colleges) or professional accreditation bodies only. Show them like this:

Thomas (Tom) Jones, BPR, MA
(613) 497-0000
Tom.Jones@gmail.com

A quick note about your choice of email address. I would suggest that you always have a professional-sounding address. A friend, whose first name is Bill and who loved playing the banjo, was using "banjobill@hotmail.com." We discussed it and agreed that, while it is nice that his personality and interests came out in the address, he was better off to switch to one that was more business-like.

Career Objective

In most cases, I would recommend that you do not include a career objective statement on your resume. This is because all the information you would include in such a statement should be clearly presented in your cover letter. Plus most employers do not read this section anyway. The only exceptions to this would be if you are trying to change your career direction or if you are entering (or re-entering) the workforce and lack experience. In both instances, your objective statement should focus on where you are going (your future) rather than where you have been (your past).

Here are a couple of examples of appropriate objective statements (if you decide to use them):

- To obtain an entry level position in the banking sector that will enable me to combine my academic knowledge and love of finance.

- To obtain a mid-level position in the tourism industry where my previous experience in advertising and public relations would be an asset.

Bear in mind that listing an objective could narrow your options to the one you have cited so be careful not to limit yourself too tightly.

Career Summary (also called Profile, Overview, Highlights)

Personally, I do not think this section is required either (for the same reasons as above). However if you do choose to include one, it should provide the reader with a quick synopsis of your qualities, accomplishments and abilities. It should be no more than three or four lines (30 – 40 words) and must grab the reader's attention.

Here are a couple of examples:

- Accomplished and versatile writer with over ten years' experience in communications. Highly-experienced in creating persuasive written communications in a variety of platforms. Excellent organizational skills with strong initiative.

- Innovative communications specialist with more than seven years' experience handling all aspects of media, public relations, internal communications, branding, and community outreach for the country's leading provider of business-to-consumer delivery.

- Professional Accountant with over 10 years' experience in investments, financial reporting, information systems and credit management. A proven ability to analyze problems, develop and simplify procedures and find innovative solutions to complex issues.

Education

If you are early in your career and education is your main selling point, you can include education at the beginning of your resume. Otherwise, it should come after your work experience as what you have done and accomplished work-wise is more interesting for employers.

Under Education, you should include all degrees, designations, certificates and diplomas granted by post-secondary institutions only. This list includes community colleges, universities and professional bodies. It does not include high school.

Typically, you would list them in reverse chronological order (most recent first) but you might consider re-arranging the order to list the ones most related to the job you are applying for first.

For example, say you've been a municipal planner for years but went back to university recently and obtained your Master in Divinity for personal rather than professional reasons. If you are applying for planning positions, you should list your planning qualifications first not your divinity degree even though it was obtained more recently.

In listing your education, you should list the correct name of your program of studies, your major (and possibly your minor) if you wish to emphasize that additional study, the name of the institution and its location (city and province). Also include your GPA (but only if it is good) and any other honours or recognition you might have received. For example:

- **Bachelor of Applied Science in Civil Engineering**
  University of Ottawa, Ottawa, ON
  Achieved 3.9 GPA; awarded University Gold Medal

- **Master of Business Administration (MBA)**
  Saint Mary's University, Halifax, NS
  Concentration in Marketing and Finance
  Achieved GPA of 3.8

If you attended a post-secondary institution but did not graduate, it is fine to include your time spent there but you must clearly indicate that you did not graduate. For example:

- **Bachelor of Arts (completed two of four years)**
  University of Saskatchewan, Saskatoon, SK

You can also use this method to describe a program of studies that is still in progress:

- **Certified General Accountant**
  Have completed Level 4 of six levels toward CGA designation
  Expected completion 2017

If you think that listing your graduation dates might work against you – because you think you're too young or too old – then leave them out. It's not necessary that you include them. However if you do decide to include them, only show the graduation year (2012) as opposed to the years you attended (2008–2012). All other programs you completed would be included in a section called Training and Professional Development.

Work Experience

Some people struggle over how to list their work history but it really is a simple, straightforward process. First, list the full corporate name of your employer, its location (city and province) and the dates of your employment (full years only). Then, you should give a brief overview of the company so the reader has a sense of what it does and its size. For example:

- **Big Food Co.,** Regina, SK   2008 - present
  Manufacturer of food products with three production facilities, 250
  employees and sales of approximately $75 million.

Next, you will list your job title, who you report to, and then three or four short lines that describe what your role is so the reader has an indication of the scope of your responsibility. Like this:

- **Business Analyst, Product Development Division**
  Report to VP Marketing. Research and analyze market potential for new product initiatives; conduct financial and economic analysis to determine feasibility; prepare written recommendations and present findings to senior management and Board of Directors.

Lastly, you will list a series of your most relevant accomplishments. They should all start with an action verb and would look something like this:

Selected accomplishments
- Developed standardized procedures to analyze all new product ideas. Process now being used company-wide.
- Conducted market analysis on chicken fingers and recommended changes to increase market acceptance. Product generated an extra $2 million in sales last year.
- Served as key member of product development team, which introduced ten new products resulting in incremental sales of $8.5 million.

If you have a long list of accomplishments, you should list the most important ones in the first two or three bullets. This is because readers often get lazy and only scan the first couple of bullets before they move onto the next section.

Remember that your work history should be listed in reverse chronological order meaning your most recent experience is listed first.

Most employers will place greater value on your more recent work history. If you have more than ten years' experience, any of the older experience should be listed but it can be considerably briefer than the current work history. In fact in many cases, you could limit this to one line only per position. Just list the company, position title and the years you held this role:

- Little Grain Company – Sales Representative   2002 – 2004

- Chicken Fingers Inc. – Inventory Coordinator   2000 – 2002

Skills

If you have a set of technical skills that are relevant to the job you're applying for, be sure to include these in a separate section. Take a look at this example taken from a Communications Advisor resume we received:

- Familiar with various social media including Facebook, Twitter, LinkedIn, Tumblr and YouTube.
- Functional in Adobe InDesign, Photoshop, Illustrator and Dreamweaver.
- Experienced with Microsoft Outlook, Word, Excel, PowerPoint, Access, Publisher and FrontPage.

Any language skills you have would be included here too.

Training and Professional Development

In this section of your resume, you should include any further learning or courses other than those listed under the Education section. For example:

- **Basic First Aid and CPR**
  St. John Ambulance

- **How to Become a Better Communicator**
  Skill Development Seminars

- **Advanced French Course (Level C)**
  Government of Canada

- **Introduction to Copy Editing**
  Ryerson University

- **Enterprise Risk & Strategic Planning**
  Risk Management & Insurance Society

A word of caution: limit your list of training to those skills that are relevant in the workplace today. For example, no one needs to know that you took a Lotus 1-2-3 course back in 1989. Listing it will only reveal your approximate age and you may get filtered out by HR staff and lose the opportunity to demonstrate your talent and skills.

Memberships

You should also list any professional or trade associations you belong to. In doing so, be sure to list any awards or forms or recognition you have received from these organizations:

- Member, Human Resources Institute of Alberta (Edmonton Chapter)

- Member, Canadian Institute of Planners

- Member, Winnipeg Chamber of Commerce
  Recipient of the Member-of-the-Year Award for overall contribution to the Chamber, 2012

Community Involvement

Depending on the type of role you are applying for, employers like to see your range of community and professional involvement. For many employers, it suggests a person with good qualities and a desire to give back to their community. This may well be a contributing factor in determining the right fit for a potential employment relationship. Your involvement can be shown like this:

- Co-Chair, Marketing Committee, Vancouver Marathon   2013, 2014

- Supervisor, Hope Food Bank Fundraiser   2012, 2013

- Volunteer, Montreal Jazz Festival   2010

This section is not date sensitive, meaning you can leave off the dates if you wish. And you can list your current and past involvements. You should exclude any involvement that might associate you with a political or religious organization unless, of course, you are applying for a job connected with one of these organizations.

Choice of politics or religion is personal and by including it on your resume, you run the risk that a potential employer will think you will bring those personal interests to work.

Personal

This is an optional section that you should include only if you feel the interests you list will add value to your application. But be careful – employers might try to read more into this than they should. For example:

Interest	Possible interpretation
Sky-diving	He's a risk-taker
Painting	She's creative
Reading	He prefers to do things on his own; he's not a team player

These interpretations may be accurate or not. That's why you have to be careful.

This is where a little research on the interviewer will help. If you learn through LinkedIn or elsewhere that the interviewer is a marathon runner and you have just completed your fifth marathon, listing this could help break the ice when you first meet. So, be careful and strategic when planning the Personal Interests sections.

Design Ideas

There are a number of rules of thumb about design that will help your resume stand out.

1. Stick to a clean typeface such as Helvetica, Arial, Calibri, Times Roman or Cambria. Your font size should be somewhere between 10 and 12 point to make it easier on the reader's eyes. Use consistent font size throughout your resume. Note – your section headings (Education, Experience and so on) may be larger but, whatever you do, be consistent in your application. And try line spacing at 1.1. It will look better with most typefaces.

    Don't forget – you should use the same typeface and font size in both your cover letter and your resume, especially if they are merged into one document and sent by email. There is a temptation to cut-and-paste sections from past resumes and letters. If you do this, always check to ensure that typeface, font size and spacing is the way you like it.

2. Your margins should be set at 1'' (or wider) all around to leave plenty of white space and be easier on the reader's eyes. I would also suggest that you

left justify the entire document. You will find that if you use full justification, large gaps between words may emerge.

3. Use bolding, underlining, initializing, or capitalizing as a way to draw attention to a heading but never use more than one of these tools at the same time. For example, it's okay to use EDUCATION but not **_EDUCATION_**. It's okay to use upper-case (capitalization) for section headings but some people use it in the body of their resume supposedly to emphasize a point, like this:

    > Achieved **RECORD** sales in my first year as sales manager. Increased overall volume from **$500,000 to $1,000,000** earning the **PRESIDENT'S AWARD** for **CONTRIBUTION TO THE COMPANY**.

    Personally, I feel this style of writing is distracting and hard to comprehend and I would recommend you avoid it.

4. A good resume is two pages in length although no one will object if it goes to a third page. There are a number of articles and books out there that will tell you to use a one-page resume only. That's fine if your experience is so senior and you are so well-established that just a line or two for each job you've held is all that is necessary. Otherwise, most resumes will require more than a page to properly explain your background.

5. Before emailing your resume to an employer, you should always save it as a PDF. That will set the format as you want it to be and will eliminate the risk of the format changing when opened by the recipient. Also, save your resume with a title that makes sense to the receiver. For example, use "Resume – Allan Ferguson" not something like "060714v2" which I have seen and received. I assume that meant July 6, 2014 (version 2) but I am not sure.

6. Finally, it's difficult to put yourself in the employer's shoes and read the resume from their perspective, but you should try your best to do that. One effective way to do this is to give the resume to someone who doesn't know you all that well. Ask them to read it and then describe how they see you. If their description is reasonably accurate, then you've done a good job drafting your resume.

What is a Functional Resume and When to Use One?

There are two formats for resumes: the chronological resume and the functional resume. The chronological resume is by far the most commonly-used format and I would say is much preferred by employers because it lists your work experience in order. It seems easier to read.

However, there are certain times when it might be better to use an alternate form of resume, known as the functional resume. The functional resume does not list your work history in any order. Rather, it groups all of your experiences and skills into "functions" and then lists what you have done and your accomplishments under each of those functions. An example of these functions might be accounting, human resources, fund raising, government relations, leadership, etc.

You should consider using a functional resume under three circumstances:

1. You are a recent graduate without a long history of work experience;
2. You are thinking about making an abrupt change in your career direction, say, from being a school teacher to being an accountant; or
3. You have been out of the workforce for a number of years and are now re-entering it.

What Not to Include on Your Resume

Reference to *Curriculum Vitae.* Avoid calling your document a "curriculum vitae" (or "CV") which looks terribly old-fashioned. You should also avoid use of résumé or resumé which almost no one uses and also looks overly traditional.

Photo. Unless you are applying for a job as a model, actor or news anchor, you should not include a photograph of yourself, even if you think you are beautiful.

References. If an employer is interested in you as a potential employee, they will ask for references later in the process. So it's best not to provide them with your resume. Plus, providing references in advance opens the door to the possibility that the employer will call one or more of these references before you even know if you really want the job. This could end up being very embarrassing for you particularly if your references are linked somehow to your current employer. You probably don't want your current employer to know that you are applying for jobs elsewhere.

You don't even have to include the standard phrase "References provided upon request" as every employer knows this is the case. Save the space.

Salary history. Any discussion about salary is best left until much later in the hiring process, ideally after you have interviewed at least once with the employer. Salary is very much a process of negotiation and revealing your salary history could put you at a significant disadvantage in the negotiation process.

An exception to this rule is if the employer specifically asks for salary expectations in the job posting. In this case, you should identify an expected salary range in your cover letter.

Age, gender, status and physical description. Not long ago, it was common to see a section on most resumes that was headed up "Personal" and went something like this:

Date of birth: April 15, 1960
Gender: Male
Status: Married with three children
Height: ·   6' 3"
Weight: 210 lbs.

Since human rights legislation prevents employers from discriminating on the basis of these items, you should exclude them from your resume. They are of no business to an employer.

Jargon or abbreviations. You do not want to do anything that might limit the reader's understanding or appreciation for your capabilities. Always use generally understood descriptions on your resume unless you are absolutely certain that the resume will be read by people who are familiar with the terminology.

Political or religious affiliation. Unless you are applying for a job within a political or religious organization, you would be wise to avoid referring to any involvement you might have with these organizations. This is because employers might believe your decision-making could be influenced by your personal beliefs.

Lies, exaggerations and embellishments. Pretty much everything you state on your resume can be checked or at a minimum, you might have to provide proof (such as educational credentials). If you are hired and it is later discovered that you were deliberately untruthful on your resume, you could be fired "for cause" which usually means you receive no notice period and no severance.

Reason why you left previous jobs. This will inevitably come up during the interview process and you should be prepared to discuss it then.

Ask Gerry

Q. I have decided to take a few years off while my children are young but anticipate re-entering the workforce maybe five or seven years down the road. Is there any strategy you would recommend I follow so I don't fall too far behind?

A. You are wise to be thinking about this, because skills that are marketable now might be obsolete by the time you re-enter the workforce. I would suggest you consider this approach. First, ensure that your skills remain current while you're out of the regular workforce. You can do this by taking courses, attending workshops, and reading material relevant to your occupation. Second, attempt to maintain as many work-related relationships as possible. This will be difficult because you will not be at work physically, but do your best to meet people for lunch, attend networking events, and connect through social media. Third, if time permits, you might consider doing part-time work from home. It will keep you sharp and help maintain (or build) those much-needed relationships.

Use Action Verbs to Craft a Powerful Resume

Your resume is, by far, the best tool you have to make you stand out from all the other people who will be applying for that same job. Remember: the purpose of a resume is to get you into the interview with the hiring manager. You can do what most people do – use boring, non-descript words that doing absolutely nothing to distinguish you from everyone else. Or you can try to make yourself stand apart from your competitors by using persuasive words, action-oriented words.

So, instead of starting each phrase with something boring and mundane like, "*Responsible for ....*", try using one of these compelling action verbs:

Accelerated	Combined	Downsized
Accrued	Communicated	Drafted
Accumulated	Compiled	Earned
Achieved	Completed	Edited
Acquired	Composed	Elevated
Acted	Computed	Eliminated
Added	Conceived	Employed
Adjusted	Concentrated	Encouraged
Administered	Concluded	Enforced
Advanced	Conducted	Enhanced
Advised	Consolidated	Enlarged
Alleviated	Constructed	Ensured
Analyzed	Consulted	Escalated
Applied	Consummated	Established
Appointed	Contracted	Estimated
Approved	Contributed	Evaluated
Arranged	Controlled	Evolved
Assembled	Converted	Examined
Assessed	Coordinated	Exceeded
Assigned	Corrected	Executed
Assisted	Counselled	Expanded
Attained	Created	Expedited
Audited	Customized	Facilitated
Authored	Decentralized	Figured
Averted	Decided	Forecasted
Avoided	Decreased	Formed
Balanced	Defined	Formulated
Bargained	Delegated	Founded
Bolstered	Delivered	Generated
Budgeted	Demonstrated	Grouped
Built	Described	Guided
Calculated	Designated	Halted
Catalogued	Designed	Headed
Centralized	Determined	Helped
Certified	Developed	Hired
Chaired	Devised	Identified
Changed	Diagnosed	Illustrated
Clarified	Directed	Impacted
Classified	Discovered	Implemented
Closed	Distributed	Improved
Coached	Documented	Improvised
Collaborated	Doubled	Increased

Influenced	Redesigned	Verified
Initiated	Reduced	Worked
Inspected	Refocused	Wrote
Installed	Renegotiated	
Instituted	Renovated	
Instructed	Reorganized	
Insured	Repaired	
Launched	Reported	
Led	Researched	
Made	Reshaped	
Maintained	Restructured	
Managed	Resulted	
Marketed	Reversed	
Mediated	Reviewed	
Merged	Revised	
Mobilized	Saved	
Moderated	Scheduled	
Modernized	Selected	
Monitored	Serviced	
Motivated	Simplified	
Negotiated	Sold	
Obtained	Solved	
Opened	Spearheaded	
Operated	Specified	
Organized	Standardized	
Participated	Started	
Performed	Stimulated	
Persuaded	Strengthened	
Planned	Structured	
Prepared	Summarized	
Presented	Supervised	
Presided	Systemized	
Produced	Tested	
Programmed	Tracked	
Projected	Trained	
Promoted	Transferred	
Proposed	Transformed	
Provided	Translated	
Purchased	Turned around	
Recommended	Upgraded	
Reconciled	Used	
Rectified	Utilized	

Chapter 10

Write a Cover Letter That Shows You're Qualified

"The resume focuses on you and the past. The cover letter focuses on the employer and the future. Tell the hiring professional what you can do to benefit the organization in the future."

- Joyce Lain Kennedy

IN OUR SEARCH practice, when I put out a job posting, I look for cover letters that do three things:

- Tell me who you are professionally;
- Explain (clearly) how your background relates to what we're looking for; and
- Contain no spelling errors, typos, or grammatical errors.

I've probably read somewhere between 50,000 and 75,000 cover letters over the course of my career. And, I can tell you the number of letters that meet these three criteria is shockingly low. This is not the time to be satisfied with "good enough." Standing out from the crowd is what you should be striving for. Let's dissect the cover letter from start to finish and talk about what should and should not be done.

How should the letter be addressed?

Do exactly as it says in the job posting. If the posting says, please respond to:

Jane Doe
Human Resources Manager
ABC Company Limited
123 Main Street
Toronto, ON L1P 4P5

Then, that's exactly how you should start your letter. Be sure to include the salutation: *Dear Ms. Doe.* Unless you know the recipient personally, do not say *Dear Jane.* And do not say, *Dear Sir or Madam* if her name is given. (Believe it or not, I have seen this even though the addressee was a woman.) If the posting says, please respond to "resumes@abc.com", you should address the letter *To Whom it May Concern.* Don't assume, as many do, that the addressee is male and say, *Dear Sirs.*

Opening paragraph

If you've been referred to this company by a mutual acquaintance, this is where you drop that person's name. For example,

> I was referred to you by Fred Smith, one of your long-time customers and a former classmate of mine. Fred suggested that my experience might be of interest to you.

Or, if you crossed paths with this person before, mention this fact as a reminder to them: ,

> You and I met briefly at the fly fishing conference last month and we had a discussion about the challenges in your industry.

If you don't have any names to "drop" your opening sentence should simply indicate the position you are applying for:

> I am writing in response to your job posting in Charity Village for an Executive Director. I have extensive experience in the not-for-profit sector and am very interested in this role. I enclose my resume for your consideration.

Body paragraph

This is the most important part of the cover letter, as it is your opportunity to link your education, experience and qualifications to the requirements the employer has listed in the posting.

There are a couple of ways to approach this. One is to match your qualifications to the employer's requirements in a two-column tabular format, like this:

Your requirements	My qualifications
Recruiting and hiring experience	Created recruitment processes that attracted over 50 new hires last year.
Administrative skills	Assisted Director in planning and directing all human resource activities including performance reviews, compensation, benefits, salary administration, budgeting and employee relations.
Real estate industry knowledge	Hold real estate brokerage licence. Completed courses in property management and real estate law.

This method makes it very easy for the employer to read and determine if you meet the minimum requirements. It is simple and straightforward.

Another way is to explain why you are qualified for the role and, if hired, how you could contribute to the success of that employer. Here is an actual advertisement we ran on behalf of a not-for-profit which was looking to hire an Executive Director, followed by one of the great cover letters we received. Both the employer and respondent have been disguised.

EXECUTIVE DIRECTOR

Goodwill House is a not-for-profit recovery residence that provides programming and services to men who are striving to overcome addictions to alcohol, drugs and gambling. The Board of Directors is now seeking an experienced Executive Director to assume a leadership role in the operation of Goodwill House and the strategic implementation of the organization's client-focused mandate.

Reporting to a Board of Directors, your responsibilities will include:

- Playing a leadership role in the advancement of the mission;
- Preparing funding applications and maintaining existing, and fostering new, relationships with governmental and non-governmental funding agencies;
- Overseeing the delivery of counselling and programming to residents;

- Managing the day-to-day operations of the organization;
- Providing leadership and supervision to staff members; and
- Providing clear and ongoing reporting to the Board with respect to operations.

As the ideal candidate, you are a service-oriented leader and team player whose strong personal values reflect those of Goodwill House. You have a proven record of providing solid leadership, ideally in the addictions recovery or other healthcare sector, although consideration will be given to candidates with relevant experience in other sectors. You have appropriate academic credentials and possess a strong blend of interpersonal qualities that include planning, communication (written and oral), fundraising, compassion for others, dispute resolution, and problem-solving skills. Salary is in the $50,000 range.

If you are interested in this important opportunity, please forward a two-page (maximum) letter explaining why you are qualified for this role and, as Executive Director, how you could contribute to the work of Goodwill House. Please also attach a resume. Submissions can be emailed to Gerald Walsh Associates Inc. at apply@geraldwalsh.com, quoting project number 1564 in the subject line.

Cover Letter Response

To Whom It May Concern:

Please consider me an applicant for the position of Executive Director for Goodwill House, position number 1564.

You will see in my resume that I moved from the casino industry into the community development and the non-profit sector. I made this move for my own mental health, after developing relationships with people in the casino and then seeing the changes in those individuals as they returned day after day to play the slot machines and ended up losing so much more than money. I comforted patrons of the casinos as they forgot to pick their children up from school; forgot to meet their sister at the airport; indeed, forgot everything but the machine in front of them. I had to harden my heart so I could continue to work, until finally a patron committed suicide and I awoke to how much I had distanced myself from the people I saw every day. I made the decision to work in a field where I could be part of the solution to this issue, rather than contribute to the problem.

My education is well-suited for this position. I received a Diploma in Human Services with a concentration in Addictions Counselling and graduated with honours. I am now working toward my Masters of Arts in Integrated Studies degree and my thesis topic is "Skinny Girl – A Systematic Targeting of Young Women by the Liquor Corporations."

Since graduation, I have remained in contact with many in the addictions field. I have helped to plan an addictions conference with professionals from across the province, and I have a very good working relationship with the Chair of the Addictions Counselling Department at my former community college. My listening skills are based in solution focused techniques with a philosophy of building upon strengths and meeting each individual with empathy and unconditional positive regard.

I have extensive experience with all aspects of operating a non-profit society. I have extensive understanding of the human resource challenges facing employees and volunteers which are vital to the sustainability of non-profits. I have seven years of experience with human resource management, and I have taken a course through the HR Council of Canada on issues specific to the non-profit sector.

I enjoy networking with community partners and stakeholders, and recognize the importance of such relationships in developing proposals and projects. Since I began working in community development, I have written successful proposals which have added over half a million dollars in core funding and project funds for non-profit organizations. I have also raised funds through events and donation requests.

I am adept at leading the daily operations of a team. My leadership philosophy is one of collaboration and empowerment. I focus on team building skills, as working at a non-profit has many unique challenges that require a supportive work environment. I enjoy assisting staff through problem solving and conflict resolution with their co-workers as well as participants to our programs.

I have worked with many boards over the past eight years, both as an employee and as a board member. I recognize the strengths and challenges of both positions. As an Executive Director, I find the relationship with board members to be of paramount importance and I believe strong communication between this position and the board is imperative to the success of a non-profit organization.

My family has been preparing to relocate to your area, and I would be able to begin a position very quickly. Thank you for your consideration.

[Name withheld]

Now, that's a good cover letter! Follow this candidate's strategy: show the potential employer that you have performed similar work in the past, that you have the skills they need, and that they can benefit from what you have to offer.

Closing paragraph

Wrap up your cover letter by expressing, once again, your interest in the position and the company, and telling them how they can contact you.

You should include the method(s) by which the employer can most easily reach you, usually your mobile number and your email address. It may be awkward for you if a potential employer calls you at work, so be discrete about offering your work number. Likewise, calls at home can be tricky if one of your young kids grabs the phone, or if a call comes in at meal time.

Here is appropriate wording for the close:

> I want to emphasize my interest in this position and would be pleased to discuss it further at your convenience. I can best be reached on my mobile 403-455-1222 or by email randy.resume@sympatico.com. Thank you for your consideration and I look forward to hearing from you.

Ask Gerry

Q. How long should my cover letter be and, assuming I reply by email, should my cover letter be in the body of the email or should I send it as an attachment?

A. A properly crafted cover letter will be at least one page long, perhaps two. You will never have to worry about boring the reader if you inject personality into your letter and focus on how you can solve the employer's needs. It helps to format the letter too by using lots of white space and properly-bolded headings.

Personally, I like to receive one document that combines the cover letter and resume. So simply merge the two together and attach them to the email. The subject line should read, "Cover letter and resume of _____(your name)". This avoids the requirement for the employer from having to open and print two documents.

Do's and Don'ts for Cover Letters

DO avoid spelling and grammar mistakes.

As Steve Pavlina, a California-based executive coach said in his October 2011 blog, "Nothing says 'loser' more than a cover letter filled with spelling and/or grammatical errors." Just think of what such mistakes say about you: that you're careless, that you don't pay attention to detail, or that you simply don't care enough.

DO present yourself professionally.

Employers do want to hire competent, confident, professional people. And the tone of your cover letter should reflect these traits. Even though you may want to leave your current employer, speak positively about your experiences there. Avoid at all costs complaining about how under-paid or unappreciated you are.

DON'T say you are the perfect candidate for the job

How many times have I read this line? There is simply no way that you can tell from a job posting that you are the perfect candidate for the job when you haven't even met with the employer yet. This says to the employer that you are impulsive, unrealistic, and brash.

DO say "you" much more than "I"

A cover letter is not an autobiography. The focus should be on how you meet the employer's needs not on how great your skills are. Tell the employer how you can help them, not why you deserve the job.

DON'T state your salary history or expectations

Remember, the main purpose of your cover letter and resume is to get you invited in for a job interview. Stating your salary expectations might be throwing up a barrier. So avoid doing so at all costs, unless asked for in the ad.

DO inject personality into your letter

If nothing else, your cover letter is a testament to how well you can write. Show some personality and humour in your writing. Be convincing as you attempt to sell yourself to the employer. And use creativity, particularly if you are applying for a job in a creative field.

BEFORE MOVING ON

1. Take a look at past cover letters and resumes you have sent to employers. Are they consistent with the principles outlined in these two chapters? How might they be improved for future applications you submit?

The Worst Cover Letter Ever

There's a lot of competition for the coveted title of Worst Cover Letter Ever. We went searching on Google and found one that fits the bill perfectly. Ironically, it was written by an individual who was applying for a job with The Daily Muse, an online career advice site. Here goes:

Hey,

You're probably reading a lot of applications. And you're probably not enjoying yourself. I'm writing this cover letter, and am not enjoying myself, either. So, let me cut to the chase.

I won't pretend that your company mission is my passion, but I do think sales are interesting, and you seem to have a strong background per your LinkedIn page. If you hire me, I'll show up for the hours you expect me to, and do what's asked, and you'll like me. Let's face it: that puts me ahead of 99% applicants already.

I graduated from (name omitted) and was well-liked there. And you know the importance of that for sales. I am willing to bet that you don't like the personality of most people who appear to be "qualified" for this entry-level position, based on the fact that if they've had the time to meet the qualifications for this job by the time they graduated college, they likely have no social skills. As someone who was voted "Life of the Party" in both high school and my fraternity, you won't have to worry about hiring some stiff loser who will poorly represent the youthful image of your company, or any other worries you might have about your new hire being a cultural fit.

You'll notice I haven't talked about what skills I have yet. Do I honestly need to? I went to an elite institution, and we all know I'd figure out how to use whatever programs you'd like me to toil away with. Working at your company doesn't take a rocket scientist, and I think we both know that, but the type of person you hire will matter, especially for your size team. Get back to me if you're looking for someone you'll actually enjoy working with.

- Name Withheld

Chapter 11

Using Social Media
to Find a Job

"We all have personal brands and most of us have already left a digital footprint, whether we like it or not. Proper social media use highlights your strengths that may not shine through in an interview or application and gives the world a broader view of who you are. Use it wisely."

- Amy Jo Martin

NOT USING SOCIAL media in your job search today is roughly the same as not using the telephone while job searching in the 1990s. It is an essential tool that has to be used smartly in order to promote yourself and to meet the right people.

Some people (mostly non-users) dismiss social media as nothing more than a bunch of people telling the world what they had for lunch. Of course, there is some of that going on and you should decide whether want to continue following those people. They might be wasting your time.

Whether you are a non-user, a marginal user, or an active user, there are two main reasons why being on social media will help your job search. The first is visibility. You have to make yourself known to employers who are increasingly using social media to find and screen candidates. The research varies on this number but upwards of 50% of employers say they use social media during the hiring process and over 90% of recruitment firms are actively engaged in using social media. Being "out there" on social media will put you on the radar of employers.

The second reason involves connecting with people. Despite all the technology, finding a job still means you have to make connections with people. That list is not limited to people who might actually hire you. It includes people who can recommend you to others, people who can help with your job search plan, and people who can build your base of knowledge. And the best way to connect with these people – especially those who you don't know already – is through social media networks.

Why an online presence matters

If you are looking for a new job now, it is especially important that you maintain a social media presence on LinkedIn, Twitter, and Facebook. But don't fool yourself: posting a profile and checking news feeds once in a while is not really considered being on social media. You have to be an active participant.

Even if you are a passive job seeker (someone who is not actively looking for a job but open to discussing good opportunities) having an online presence will make you visible to those employers who are scanning social networking sites, particularly LinkedIn, to look for candidates who could possibly be enticed to apply for a job.

As a recruiter, I use LinkedIn all the time to identify possible candidates (or passive job seekers). Once I identify someone who appears to have the qualifications I am seeking, I then "connect" with them hoping they will accept my request. Once that happens I am free to send them a message about specific job openings I may have. This may or may not result in the person actually applying for the job but either way, the process is a valuable tool for me (and all employers) to identify potential candidates.

Beyond identifying a list of possible candidates, employers use social media networks to learn more about applicants who have already applied and who may be close to receiving a job offer. Previously, the final stage before a job offer was checking references. If these "checked out" an offer was usually made. Reference checking plays an important role in the selection process and is still done by most employers. However a growing number of employers also check out finalist applicants on social media to gain insight into your character, personality and even your personal life.

The reason employers are checking sites like Facebook, Twitter, and LinkedIn is to get a better indication of who you are beyond the resume, cover letter, interview and references. The rationale for this is sound: Often candidates are very scripted in the interview. Answers can be well-rehearsed and crafted to give the employer the "answer they are looking for." In many cases, the real person does not emerge.

Checking out a candidate on social media, however, does offer the employer an opportunity to learn more about you and get a real view of you as a person.

Don't worry, employers are not always looking for "dirt" on you. Many are trying to determine if you are a good fit for their corporate culture and to see how you present yourself professionally. Some are attempting to measure your range of interests to see how well-rounded you are. Some are even looking to see how many followers you have and to view what others are saying about you.

In doing so, some employers may also learn more about other qualifications you may have for the job that did not come up during the interview.

The bottom line is that everything about you on social media should reflect favourably on you, including what other people might post. Ask yourself these questions:

- Does the content on all platforms work to your advantage?
- Does it position you professionally?
- Does it highlight your accomplishments and qualifications in a positive way?
- If you were a serious candidate for a job, would you be proud if an employer viewed everything about you?

Clean up your digital dirt

On the flip side, there clearly are things an employer could find that will turn them against hiring you. Inappropriate photos, offensive comments, or evidence of excessive drinking or drug use have been known to destroy a person's chance of getting a job offer. Likewise, poor communication skills, making disparaging remarks about former employers, and evidence that you lied about your qualifications will quickly torpedo your candidacy. Even a silly photo or stupid profile name can work against you.

So, before you embark on a job search, do an Internet search of yourself and see what comes up. But don't restrict yourself to Google – check a few search engines. And don't limit yourself to just your proper name. Check your full name and the shortened version of it (Thomas and Tom) and check it also with your middle initial.

If you find any digital dirt that you wouldn't want a potential employer to know about, get rid of it right away, if you can. If it's on someone else's site, ask that they delete it. And set up a Google alert which will notify you if any new content about you is posted.

Being invisible on line will work against you

Being silent or invisible online could very well work against you, especially if you are young job seeker. As we learned earlier, most employers will Google you if you are a serious candidate for a job. I would be concerned that if they find nothing on you on any sites it will trigger alarm bells and make them wonder if you are trying to hide something.

Even if you are not trying to hide anything but simply don't have an online presence, you risk coming across as old-fashioned and outdated. This could lead to the employer wondering about how current your skills are and they may decide to hire someone else who seems more up-to-date.

Likewise, some people attempt to hide their online presence by setting up their profiles under various nicknames or aliases. While this may work for a while, it may eventually catch up with you with embarrassing results.

Most sites have privacy settings that you should use to limit the content you want to share only with family and friends. It is smart to monitor these settings frequently as some sites are constantly changing the rules and these could impact what others are able to see about you.

The best strategy to follow is to assume that nothing is private and keep all your profiles and sites professional in appearance and content.

Connect with potential employers

Another important advantage of being active on social media is the ability to gather information on companies you are interested in, and to connect with the "right" people within those organizations.

Let's face it: finding the names and contact information of the right people to connect with is very difficult if you follow the traditional method of looking through their web site. All job search experts will tell you about the value of connecting with the decision-maker in an organization. The problem is: the decision-maker's name and information are usually difficult to locate when you browse through the company's web site. In most cases, the web site directs you to the human resources department by way of a virtually anonymous email address like: *hr@companyname.com*. You have no idea where it is going and who is receiving it.

This is where LinkedIn, in particular, is useful. All you have to do is search for all employees working for the particular company you are targeting. In all likelihood, the name of the manager you are trying to reach has a LinkedIn profile and by connecting with her you will increase your chances of getting on her radar.

Remember at this stage you are really trying to attract interest from employers rather than chasing jobs. Once you connect with the right person, you should then start producing content such as recommending relevant books or articles, contributing to online discussions, noting conferences or events that are coming up, endorsing companies and people, or just simply blogging about pertinent topics. In the eyes of your followers, you will appear interesting and up-to-date on current issues. And you will be seen as a "contributor" rather than somebody who's only in it for personal gain. You should also make regular updates to your status so that you stay top of mind.

More rules to remember about social media and job searching

1. Put yourself in the employer's shoes and think about how people are going to find you using the web. The most obvious way is to Google yourself and see how easy it is to find you. Are you happy with the results? If you're not, try to take some action that will improve your image.

2. Be sure that your profile is professional and employer-focused. Use a good photo of yourself and an appropriate name. Your profile at a minimum should outline your work history, accomplishments, qualifications, and what you can offer future employers.

3. Create networks with others in your industry by joining groups and following people who appear to be thought leaders and active on social media. Then grow your presence within your network by contributing relevant content. And don't forget to maintain these networks even after you've secured a new job.

4. Figure out your brand – how you want others to think of you? To find the right brand, you will need to spend some time determining what makes you unique. Do you have special skills that others don't have? Is your experience distinctive? Are you an exceptional communicator? Everything

that readers see and read on your profile and your posts should support your brand and the career direction you want to move in.

5. Never lie, mislead or omit important information. The resume you submitted for a particular job should always be consistent with your social media profiles. Don't give an employer any reason for ruling you out of the competition. And always be open and honest about your employment status. There is nothing unusual about being unemployed.

6. It goes without saying (but I will repeat it anyway), make sure your profile and all your online postings are free from grammatical errors, foul language and typos.

7. Check your privacy settings but don't become too restrictive. Remember the idea behind social media is that information is shared. You don't want to make it too difficult for an employer to locate information on you, otherwise you might miss a good opportunity.

8. Be a contributor of content and not someone who is chasing a job. You do this by posting articles, joining social networking groups, participating in group discussions, and generally sharing your knowledge and expertise with others in your network. This more subtle approach will attract more job opportunities than coming right out and asking for work.

BEFORE MOVING ON

1. If you are already a user, take some time and review your social media presence and your public profile. Are your security settings as you want them to be? Does it present you in the way you want to be seen by employers?

2. If you are not active on social media, you must start to build a presence soon. Watch an online tutorial. Take a course. Read a book. Whatever it is, get going quickly. As I said at the beginning of this chapter, not being on social media now is like not using the telephone for your job search in the 1990s.

Chapter 12

Choose Your References Carefully

"Promise me you'll always remember: You're braver than you believe, stronger than you seem, and smarter than you think."

- A.A. Milne

EVEN THOUGH SOME people downplay the value of reference checking, most employers will still check the references of candidates they are considering hiring. Here are some of the questions I've been asked about selecting and presenting references.

Who should be on my list?

I think it is always best to have a long list of potential references, perhaps as many as seven or eight people, even though you will only have to provide three or four names in the end. If you have more than you need, you can then select the best ones for that particular job opportunity.

I would not bother with providing personal references, such as friends or relatives, as employers do not place any weight on what they would say. They are certainly in no position to provide work-related information about your background.

You should only provide professional references – those individuals who can attest to your past work experience. They are the ones who are most knowledgeable of your work habits, interpersonal qualities and skill levels.

One possible exception to this rule might be providing the name of a reference who serves with you, say, on an outside Board or committee. While this role may not be related to your work directly, you will often display work-like qualities when performing the duties of that function, particularly if you are in a leadership role.

Clearly, you should only select references who you know will provide you with a favourable reference. This is not to say that they won't speak about some of your weaknesses. But overall you must be confident they will say good things about you.

How do I know what my references will say about me?

That's simple – ask them! It's no good just to get permission to use their name. You must follow up and ask, "If Company X calls you, what will you say about me?" It's a fair question.

This is a great opportunity for you to coach your references. I am not saying that you will be able to put words in their mouths. But you might be able to craft how they will speak about you, or refresh their memory about your past accomplishments. Memories fade quickly and a past employer might forget how you helped out on a key project several years ago.

Of course, another key advantage of asking a past employer what they would say about you is to weed out the ones who will say negative things about you. You may be wondering if this can possibly happen. Believe me, it does. I have spoken with dozens of references over the years who have responded with something like, "I don't understand how they could possibly have given you my name as a reference, as there is nothing positive I can say about them." Yes, it happens.

Should I attach references to my resume when applying?

No. If an employer is interested in you possibly working for their company, they will ask for references later in the process. Plus, providing references in advance opens the door to the possibility that the employer will call one or more of these references before you even know if you really want the job. This could end up being embarrassing for you, particularly if your references are linked somehow to your current employer. You probably don't want your current employer aware that you are applying for jobs elsewhere.

How should I present my references?

You want to make things as easy as possible for the reference-checker by giving them not only the reference's name but their current title and position, their relationship to you, and all their contact information. Here is how you might present the information to make the task easier for them:

Name:	Martha Lee
Position:	Chief Financial Officer
	ABC Technology Company
Address:	2876 Main Street
	Winnipeg, MB R3C 1A6
Email:	Martha.Lee@bell.ca
Telephone:	204-123- 4567 (work)
	204-890-9876 (cell)
Relationship:	My former manager

How can I coach my references?

Once a potential employer has asked you for a list of references, you can assume they will be checking them. But before they do, you should contact them to inform them about the job you've applied for. Tell them about the company, its issues, what the job involves and its responsibilities, and what the company is looking for in possible candidates, and why the job appeals to you.

You should also give them a list of possible interview questions they might be asked. There is no guarantee they will be asked these questions but briefing them fully in advance allows your references some time to think about how your past experience will suit you well for this job. You will benefit from this approach.

What questions will the references be asked?

For the most part, the reference questions will be driven from the job description or advertisement. That's why it is helpful if you send the actual job posting to each of your references. Here is an excerpt from an ad for an Executive Director search we completed for a professional association in the health care sector.

> Reporting to a Board of Directors, you will be responsible for providing advice and direction on strategic and policy matters. With a new strategic plan in place, the organization is poised to be the leader in educating residents about the importance of life-long health and, as Executive Director, you will play a key role in continuing the plan's implementation.
>
> As Executive Director, you will also maintain effective relationships with government and other key stakeholders to advocate for the interests of the profession. Operationally, you will oversee all day-to-day functions of the association including member services, human resources, public affairs, media relations, finances, and administration. You will also liaise regularly with your peers across Canada in the various provincial and national

associations as you work closely together on matters of strategic importance to the profession.

As the ideal candidate, you are a strategic, collaborative leader with a proven track record in professional association management. You have a thorough understanding of governance processes and have an interpersonal style that promotes cooperation and understanding among stakeholders. Strong in government relations and advocacy roles, you are an excellent communicator who can build consensus with people and groups to meet challenging objectives. Ideally, you have an understanding of current and emerging issues within the health care sector and possess relevant academic and professional qualifications.

Based on this set of responsibilities and requirements, these are the reference questions we asked. Let's assume the candidate's name is Steve.

- Can you tell how you know Steve and describe your previous working relationship with him?
- When was Steve employed with your organization?
- In this role, Steve would be expected to demonstrate strategic leadership in all facets of the job. Can you comment on his leadership qualities and tell me of any times when he has demonstrated strong leadership?
- One of the key aspects of this job is government relations. In order to ensure the continued sustainability and growth of the association and its members, the association must maintain good relationships with governments. Could you describe how effective Steve would be in the area of government relations?
- A critical component of the Executive Director's is to ensure that all members, receive value for their membership? Do you have a sense of how Steve would be in the member services area?
- The job also involves managing a small staff. Based on your knowledge of Steve, are you able to comment on his coaching, mentoring and supervisory abilities?
- Could you describe Steve's interpersonal style, particularly in the context of how he might relate to various stakeholders such as members, government, other health associations, and the general public?
- How did Steve get along with his co-workers?
- Can you comment on Steve's organizational and planning abilities?
- What would say are Steve's shortcomings?
- What was Steve's reason for leaving your company?
- Would you re-hire Steve if given the opportunity?
- Is there anything else you would like to add or anything else we should know about Steve that would be helpful?

BEFORE MOVING ON

1. Give serious thought to who you are choosing as references. This is not an insignificant part of the job searching process. Make sure your references are work-related (possibly including volunteer work) and that they will give a fair and honest assessment of your skills, abilities and accomplishments.

Jennie's Story

Jennie King knew at an early age that she wanted to do something creative. She didn't know what it was but by sticking to her guiding principles, she has managed to achieve just that.

Q: What was your early career like?
A: I was raised in an entrepreneurial family but unlike some others in my family, who became accountants, I was the creative one. I always knew I was going to do something related to marketing in the creative sector. I was fortunate to get my first job right out of school with a company that manufactured oceanographic equipment. Honestly, for the first six months I couldn't understand what they did and was thinking of leaving. Then, it all became clear to me and I began to understand what an impact they were making on ocean science. While this job wasn't exactly creative, it was a good first step for me.

What did you learn from that first job?
What I learned at a young age was that it was very important to me to work for a great company. It doesn't have to be large but it has to value its employees and provide lots of opportunity for growth.

What happened after that?
After being there for eight or nine years, I started to become bored and wanted a more creative environment. Also, I was in my early 30s and had a young family, so the travel was getting harder and harder. I ended up joining a radio station thinking I would have more flexibility and would be able to use my creative and marketing side more. But I was there only a few days when I realized it was not the kind of environment I wanted to be in. Most of what the company said to me in the interview turned out to be inaccurate, including how they dealt with people. I guess I could have vetted them better in the interview but I was naïve and believed what they told me. I left within a year.

Where did you go?

I was very lucky to get on with a professional theatre company, initially in a marketing and sponsorship role. I have since become their Director of Sales and Marketing where I oversee things like public relations, corporate sponsorships, donor development, ticket sales, and community outreach and programming. I am also involved in preparing marketing and sales plans, and I manage the relationships with media, sponsors, donors, and other arts partners. I am so proud of our brand in the community and it is nice to represent them.

Do you love your job?

Yes. I never dread going to work. I can remember times in the past when I hated Mondays and couldn't wait until Fridays. That's not the case anymore. I also love being surrounded by artists who bring out the creative in me and I love working for a company that respects its employees. When I see a lot of my friends who are stuck in their careers and just working to pay the bills, I realize how lucky I am.

Section Three

The Search

"Fall seven times, stand up eight."

–Japanese proverb

Chapter 13

Job Hunting Myths

**"If you tell the truth,
you don't have to remember anything."**

- Mark Twain

EVERY DAY I witness intelligent people make serious mistakes when they look for a job. And this doesn't just apply to young people entering the job market for the first time. I see candidates for very senior-level jobs write inadequate resumes, prepare poorly for interviews and present themselves badly in front of prospective employers.

Frankly, it puzzled me for years why smart people kept making the same mistakes when it came to looking for jobs. But then it finally struck me: there are certain well-kept secrets about the real way people get jobs. Yet it is also true that many job-seekers fall into the trap of what I call "job hunting myths" that restrict their ability to find a meaningful job.

Here are the ten biggest job-hunting myths I hear most often followed by the job market *reality*:

1. If I apply for all kinds of different jobs, it will increase my chances of getting one.

Wrong! Employers can easily spot a general, mass application and they don't like them. You should be selective and apply only for those jobs for which you meet the qualifications and criteria. Employers appreciate applicants who have taken the time to research their organization and who have demonstrated why they would be good in the particular role.

2. I've sent my resume to a number of recruiting firms – one of them will find me a job.

Wrong! While you could find a job through a recruiter, you must remember that recruiters are hired by employers to fill their job openings. The employer is the client, not you. Recruiters will only recommend you to an employer if they think you are a strong fit for that employer's needs.

3. I am over 50 and worried that my age will be a problem.

Wrong! Age is much less of a factor than it used to be as the younger population shrinks and older folks stay healthier and work longer. The important question is whether you have the skills, education and experience the employer is seeking. Also, many employers like to hire older workers because they believe they will stay longer and are more reliable. So unless you are looking for a career as a supermodel or firefighter, don't be obsessed with your age.

4. I can't network because I don't have many contacts.

Wrong! While it is true that it easier to find a job if you know a lot of people, you can easily approach people you don't know and ask them for advice on their career, company and industry. And if you have the right background for roles in their company, they will almost certainly consider you even if they don't already know you.

5. It's a lot easier looking for a job if I have a job.

Wrong! Almost everyone has been downsized at one time or another so there is no longer a stigma attached to being unemployed. Think of how many of your friends, relatives and former co-workers have lost their job through no fault of their own.

In fact, if you can afford it, it could even be worthwhile to leave a job that you are not happy in so that you can work full time trying to find the right job.

6. The best-skilled candidate will always get the job.

Wrong! Just because you have all the skills an employer is seeking, it doesn't mean you will get a job offer. Employers also look for "fit" and the ability to learn. The truth is many employers will choose someone with fewer skills and a great attitude over someone with all the skills, but who seems hard to get along with.

7. I am having trouble finding a job – something is wrong with my resume.

Wrong! People spend far too much time fussing over their resume by continually updating and modifying it. No question – you need a well-written resume and should invest time at the beginning of your search ensuring that it is accurate, thorough and professional. But you will see your greatest return by reaching out to your personal connections and meeting as many people as possible.

8. I have changed jobs a lot. That will work against me.

Wrong! This hasn't been a problem since the so-called "loyalty bond" between employers and employees was broken during the recession of the early 1990s. Employers understand that a traditional career path with one employer is a thing of the past and that people have to change jobs a lot to advance their careers. You might want to avoid really short stays in a job, say, under a year, but otherwise don't worry about moving around.

9. Nothing happens over the summer and the holidays.

Wrong! People think that all hiring ceases in July, August and December and that job searching during these periods is a waste of time. The truth is that people leave their jobs at all times of the year, so always stay active in the job hunt. In fact, try stepping up your activity during slow times – it may be easier to see the people you want.

10. I don't bother sending a cover letter. No one reads it anyway.

Wrong! You don't know what value the employer places in the cover letter. Some will read it carefully; others will ignore it. Many overlook this step. A well-written cover letter gives you an opportunity to explain why you are interested in and qualified for the job, and shows the hiring manager that you have taken the time to research their organization.

BEFORE MOVING ON

1. What are some of the strongly-held beliefs you hold that prevent you from moving ahead with your job search? How reasonable are these beliefs?

Ask Gerry

Q. I really want to change jobs but just can't seem to get started, mostly because I lack the time to devote to a job search. I work long hours (which is one of the reasons I want to change) and when I get home, my kids demand my time and attention. How would you suggest a busy person like me approach a job search?

A. Your desire to change jobs will remain just a dream until you take action. It's like hoping to get fit without exercising. It won't happen. You simply must find time to spend on your search, otherwise you will end up staying right where you are. There are a few things you might consider to find more time and to become more productive with the time you have. Start to identify the time-wasters in your life, like Facebook and other social media, video games and television, and eliminate them. Get up an hour earlier when you can probably work uninterrupted or set aside blocks of time, like Sunday afternoon, to work on your search activities. If it's difficult working at home, find a place where you can work productively, like the library or a coffee shop, and consider that your personal "office." You might also check out hiring a career coach and meet with that person regularly. The built-in accountability of working with an unbiased coach will help keep you on track.

Chapter 14

The Marketing Mindset

*"Always set your goals higher than you could ever possibly reach.
That way, when you barely fall short, you're still better than everybody else."*

— Carson V. Heady, *Birth of a Salesman*

NOW THAT THESE myths have been (hopefully) debunked, it is time to understand that searching for a job is essentially the same as marketing almost any service or product.

As the "seller", what you possess is a unique set of qualifications, skills and experience that you are "offering" to an employer, the potential buyer. If that employer has a need for your services then they will "buy" what you are offering and pay you for it – your salary!

This is what is known as the exchange process. One party, the seller, provides a product needed by another party, the customer. In return, the customer gives back something of value, usually money. In the end, both parties receive something of value.

If you want to be successful in your job search, understanding the value of marketing, and how to apply those same principles that companies have used for years to sell their products, will be essential.

The Marketing Mix Applied to Job Seekers

The definition of marketing that many specialists use is: *Putting the right product in the right place, at the right price, at the right time.* Now I don't remember much from my years studying business in university but one concept that I do recall is the 4Ps of marketing – Product, Promotion, Place and Price.

The 4Ps of marketing is often thought of as the "marketing mix" and you can easily apply this concept to your job search and use it as a framework for thinking about how to approach different aspects of searching for a job.

Product. The product is you or more accurately, it is the unique blend of education, training, work experience, personal qualities, skills and capabilities that makes you stand out from others in the eyes of employers. Your job is to know what is on that list, which is easier said than done, and more importantly how you can communicate that list to others. In marketing, this is often referred to as the Unique Selling Proposition (USP). No matter how attractive a product you are, employers may not recognize and value you unless you can properly communicate your USP.

Be sure you can answer these questions succinctly:

> What are your accomplishments (not duties or job titles)?
> What strengths and skills do you bring to an employer?
> What makes you different from other job seekers?
> What is your competitive advantage?
> Why should an employer hire you?
> How can you add value to the employer?

Promotion. When job searching, "promotion" means anything that you can use to help you get to the job interview and ultimately get a job offer. This includes cover letters, resumes, social media presence, telephone calls, connecting with people, building relationships and interviewing.

As you saw in Section Two (The Toolbox), these tools all have to be sharp and are considered by many experts to be the most important piece of the career marketing mix. No matter how good your "product" is, you will not get the job if you cannot properly communicate your qualities to prospective employers.

Good marketers will attempt to reach (or touch) as many possible buyers of their goods as possible. Similarly, the goal for you in job searching is to be as broad as possible in your reach. One of the steps you should undertake is to determine how many contacts you want to make each week. It is not unreasonable for you to make five, ten, or even fifteen contacts per week. While this number may seem high, especially if you are currently employed and looking for another job, you can easily generate a large list of contact names. This list includes not just companies that might hire you but also friends, referral sources, colleagues and past employers. One thing to bear in mind is that there is usually a direct correlation between the number of qualified contacts you make and the number of interviews granted.

Place. In a business context, "Place" refers to the channels you choose to distribute product to your customers. Is your product sold in retail outlets, online, by catalogue, or a sales force? In job searching, how you distribute product (you) to potential employers has to be considered carefully. So many people rely solely on responding to published openings on job boards and various websites. While this is one of the channels you should explore, unfortunately it only amounts to about 20% of job openings.

As you will see in the following chapters, you have to rely on building your own personal connections, where the greatest number of job leads will be, plus contacting companies directly and building relationships with recruiters who might specialize in your field.

In exploring these channels, you should understand another important marketing concept called *frequency of message.*

Good marketers know that people need to be told something several times before they will remember it automatically. That's why you see advertisements shown repeatedly on the same show. Or why sales people continue to call even though you do not have a need for their product now. According to the online marketing site, *The Marketing Donut*, persistence pays off. They claim that almost no one buys on the first call and that 80% of sales occur only after *five* calls or more. But by then, most callers – they say 92% – have given up! What this means, then, is that just 8% of sales people are getting 80% of sales. These exact same principles apply to the job search process. You must be persistent and frequent in your messaging.

Price. When companies consider how to set their selling price, they ask themselves a number of questions:

> What is the perceived value of our product (or service) to the buyer?
> What does it cost us to produce the product?
> What prices will our competitors charge?
> Will offering a discount increase our market share?
> Might we be able to increase our margin by pricing higher?

You should apply this same way of thinking when it comes to setting your salary expectations and negotiating salary. I am a strong proponent of thinking about "total compensation" and not just base salary. That means focusing on all aspects of the package including cash compensation (salary, bonuses, pension contributions, benefit coverage, profit sharing, memberships, etc.) as well as non-cash compensation (vacation, personal days, sick leave, flex-days, working from home, etc.) You will find a lot more about this topic in Section Five: The Job Offer.

BEFORE MOVING ON

1. Take a few moments and put yourself in the marketing mindset. Using the 4Ps of marketing (Product, Promotion, Place and Price), prepare a summary of how these apply to you and your job search.

Ask Gerry

Q. How long will my job search take?

A. Even though this question is on the mind of most job seekers, there is no way to answer with precision. However, one thing is certain. We tend to under-estimate the amount of time it will take us to get anything done. So, be realistic in your expectations. Even the shortest job search will take between two and three months as it takes at least that amount of time for a company to post an ad, interview candidates, check references, convey an offer and then bring the person on board.

Other factors that can influence the amount of time it takes to find a job include your level of seniority, salary expectations, your network of contacts, demand for your skills, and most importantly, the level of effort you put into your search. Although some people fall into jobs by good luck, I am convinced that the harder you work at finding a job, the quicker you will find one. This is particularly relevant if you are out of work now. If this is the case, you should be willing to devote full-time hours to finding a new job.

Chapter 15

Using Your Personal Connections
to Generate Leads

"I don't think of (building personal connections) as cold and impersonal, the way I thought of networking. Instead, I was connecting – sharing my knowledge, resources, time and energy … in a continual effort to provide value to others. Like business itself, being a connector is not about managing transactions, but about managing relationships."

- Keith Ferrazzi, *Never Eat Alone*

MOST PEOPLE HATE networking, or at least the term "networking." For example, when I ask participants in my job search workshops what comes to mind when I say "networking" or "networker," they come up with words like ruthless, big-talker, gossiper, slick, devious, tricky, disingenuous, and a bunch of other words I can't repeat here.

No one wants to be thought of as the insincere glad-hander you find at networking events. You know, the fellow who presses a business card into your hand while he looks over your shoulder for someone else more important to talk to.

That is why I have *not* done what most authors of job search books have done and call this section "networking." To me, building personal connections is much different, and more effective, than traditional networking. Building personal connections, something you should be doing continuously, is more about developing meaningful relationships with others that are characterized by give-and-take. This means that the relationship is mutual and of value to both parties involved. As Ferrazzi said in his book, "Today's most valuable currency is social capital" which he defines as the "information, expertise, trust and total value that exists in a relationship."

"It's Not What You Know But Who You Know"

Everybody is familiar with this old saying. And believe me – it's alive and well in the career industry.

In survey after survey, it's reported that roughly half of all jobs are found through some form of personal connection. That person might be your next-door neighbour or a distant acquaintance. But regardless, they are part of a social network that you and I and everyone else have around us. So, who are these people?

I am willing to bet that your list is a longer than you think. In fact, I am confident you can come up with at least 100 names or more pretty quickly. Let's start with this list:

Family members	Club members
Friends	Community leaders
Friends of friends	Lawyer
Friends of your parents	Doctor
Parents of your children's friends	Dentist
Relatives	Accountant
Neighbours	Realtor
Former classmates	Banker
Old teachers	Financial advisor
Professors	Insurance agent
Coaches	Health club members
Past employers	Alumni
Clients	Church members
Suppliers	Service club members
Co-workers	

Start by writing down the names of people who fall into these groups. To simplify the task, you might categorize them this way:

Level 1 connections: People you have a close connection with and see frequently such as family, friends, and neighbours.

Level 2 connections: People you would describe more as work-related colleagues and associates.

The reason these categories are relevant was brought out in a well-known study by Mark Granovetter, an American sociologist and professor at Stanford University, called *The Strength of Weak Ties.* Granovetter reported that job seekers were more likely to find jobs from leads and information passed along to them by people to whom they were not particularly close. This contradicts the widely-held belief that those closest to you will be the most help to you in finding a job.

When Granovetter measured the strength of social ties between job seekers and the people giving them the lead, he found that of those who found jobs through personal connections :

- Only 17% saw their contact "often,"
- 56% saw their contact "occasionally," and
- 28% saw their contact rarely.

His conclusions? The people in your life who you know but not too well (aka "the weak ties") are the ones who will help you the most in your job search. To use our categories, Level 1 would be considered your "strong ties" and Level 2 your "weak ties."

The main reason Granovetter concludes that your best job leads come from your weak ties (Level 2) is that they move in circles you don't. They work in different sectors, socialize with different people, and know about different job opportunities than you do.

On the flip side, your strong ties (your Level 1 contacts) move in the same circles as you and there's a high probability you already know about or will uncover the same job leads as they will.

However you must not overlook the very significant role your Level 1 contacts play in your job search. This is the group that will help you through tough times. Since you know them best, it's the group that will give you honest feedback on your resume, help you with practice interviews, empathize with you when you don't get the offer you hoped for, and boost your confidence at times when you need it most.

Your Level 1 contacts are really on your team. They are those people who are a meaningful part of your life and they will play an instrumental role in helping you through the search process. Always remember to show your gratitude to them and let them know how important they are to you.

You Still Have To Be Good At What You Do

I said earlier, "It's not what you know but who you know." While there's truth in that statement, I don't want you to take it out of context – you still have to be good at what you do.

That's because if a personal connection – even your favourite cousin – is recommending you for a job in their company or another company, they are putting their own personal reputation at risk. By helping you and passing your name along to someone else, they are in fact saying you are a good person and capable of doing the job. If you get hired and somehow screw up down the road, they will look bad and their own reputation will be damaged.

So, remember, just because you know somebody, it doesn't mean they will automatically go to bat for you. You may have to convince them that you can do a good job. That will reduce the perceived risk for them and hopefully convince them to recommend you for the job.

The Hidden Job Market

Your personal connections, particularly the Level 2 ones, will help you the most by exposing you to the hidden job market. Not everyone understands what the hidden job market is and how large it is.

Simply put, it is all those jobs (or potential jobs) that have yet to be publicized. It contains:

- Jobs that are still in the planning stages;
- Jobs that will arise due to corporate reorganization or restructuring;
- Jobs that will open up due to retirements, resignations, promotions, or transfers;

- Jobs that arise because someone has been dismissed suddenly;
- Jobs that will arise due to expansion plans or acquisitions;
- Jobs that have been sent to a search firm but have yet to "hit the street";
- Jobs that are intended to be advertised in the future; and
- Jobs that will never be advertised because the employer prefers to hire by word of mouth.

Ask Gerry

Q. I am in the process of looking for a job and all my friends tell me I have to have an "elevator pitch." Can you help?

A. An "elevator pitch" is a 20 – 30 second speech that explains who you are, what you do (or have done), and how you might help the listener solve her problems. In your job search, there will be many opportunities for you to deliver your pitch: in the interview, at social functions, and, yes, even in elevators! Remember: your goal should be to interest the listener and focus on their needs so that you will be invited to speak to them again, perhaps in a meeting or even an interview. Here's an example of an elevator pitch:

"My name is Fred Beancounter. I am a CPA with almost twenty years' experience in accounting and financial roles in professional services, distribution and manufacturing. I have wide-ranging skills but I have been particularly successful in helping troubled companies get turned around by identifying areas for cost savings, looking for inefficiencies, raising additional capital, and streamlining their operations. In my last two roles, I have assisted these companies move from near-bankruptcy to become highly successful. I am now looking for another opportunity where I can help another organization become more profitable."

No one knows exactly how large the "hidden job market" is but most career experts suggest it is large: some say it is around 40% of total job vacancies; others estimate it as high as 80%. No matter if it's at the lower or higher end of the range, it is a big number and you should focus a lot of your time and attention trying to tap it.

The reason there is such a large hidden job market is that most employers, all things being equal, still prefer to hire someone who is known to them, even tangentially. If you are an employer and an employee, supplier, customer or close friend recommends someone to you, you will view this as less risky than hiring a complete stranger. And frankly, no matter what you say, business is still about people. Whether it is selling or hiring, it doesn't matter. People prefer to do business with people they know and like.

And there's another benefit to the employer: if they can successfully hire this way, they avoid the hassle of advertising the job, handling telephone inquiries, screening resumes, and interviewing dozens of candidates.

That is why you must access your connections to tap the hidden job market. The law of probability says that the more people you connect with, the more career opportunities you will see. For that reason alone, you should do everything you can to build your personal connections and increase the number of people who might be willing to help you in your search efforts.

You will find that the stronger (and bigger) your list gets, the more valuable it becomes and the faster it grows. That's why Keith Ferrazzi says your connections are like a muscle – "the more you work it, the bigger it gets."

How to Connect With People

With rare exceptions, you must build relationships with your personal connections in person. I know how tempting it is to sit back and rely on email. It's simple and supposedly efficient. But it's not very effective. Your contacts will respond better and invest more time in helping you when you have gone to some effort. So, use the telephone, meet with people in person, or go to their office. The more visible you are to them, the more memorable you will be.

Your Level 1 connections. This group can be contacted very easily. Since you are close to them and see them fairly often, it's not unusual for you to invite them over for dinner, out to lunch or for a coffee. In almost all cases, they will accept your invitation. The only caveat I would raise about dealing with your Level 1 connections is, because they care for you so much, they may not always give you the straight truth. That's because they don't want to hurt you.

For example, if you ask if your resume looks good, they may say "yes" even if they think it needs a lot of improvement. Or they may encourage you to apply for a particular job when in reality you don't have any chance of getting it and applying would be a complete waste of your time. To avoid receiving inaccurate feedback from your Level 1 connections, simply tell them that you want the "straight goods" – even if it hurts. You will be much better off in the long run.

Your Level 2 connections. These connections may be a little more challenging to reach. The reason for this is that there may be people on that list who you have not had contact with for several years, such as past employers, professors from your college years, and former classmates. Even though you know them (and they will probably remember you) don't assume they will automatically accept your invitation to get together.

Most people I have worked with are most comfortable with a two-step approach to these connections. The first step is to send an email re-connecting with these individuals and offering a brief explanation for the email. The second step is to follow-up with a telephone call (usually 4-5 days later) to have a brief discussion leading (hopefully) to a face-to-face meeting.

Here is a sample introductory email for your reference:

> **Subject**: Might we be able to speak?
>
> Hello Angela,
>
> It's Kathryn O'Brien here. You may remember me from our days together in the public relations industry.
>
> I wanted to re-introduce myself to you and let you know that I am exploring new professional opportunities in the marketing and PR field. Recently, I served as Director of Public Relations for a major hospital and sat on the executive leadership team. Prior to that I worked for a large telecommunications company and in public relations consulting, where our paths would have crossed.
>
> With reorganization happening in the health system, I am now looking for a new opportunity and was wondering if I could arrange to meet with you to get your thoughts on options in the market?
>
> I would appreciate any advice you may be able to provide, and will contact you next week to discuss the possibility of arranging a meeting. Thank you for your time.
>
> Kathryn

Note a few things about this communication:

1. It's brief and to the point (less than 150 words).
2. Kathryn presents a good overview of her experience – not too long but enough to demonstrate her level of experience.
3. She doesn't enclose a resume. (I think it's a good idea to make the reader want more.)
4. Kathryn states that she will take the next step. She doesn't ask Angela to respond to her.

So, what happens next? Between now and next week, when Kathryn said she would call, she is going to have to prepare a telephone script to use when she gets Angela on the phone. The best way to do this is to find out as much information as she can about the company Angela works for and the key challenges it faces, and then be able to describe how she could help them deal with those issues.

The reason for this is she may not be able to get a face-to-face meeting and so she should be prepared for a mini telephone interview just in case. She should also list the outcomes she would like to achieve from the call. Her goal is a face-to-face interview but failing that she should seek the names of two or three referrals and the answers to certain questions.

Kathryn will also have to think about the timing of her call to Angela to get the best results. She might want to think about early morning, over the noon hour or at the end of the day as these will be the times she will most likely get through to her.

If Kathryn calls and it goes through to voice mail, she should have a short script ready to remind Angela who she is and to give a brief synopsis of her background and reason for the call. She should never leave her number and ask Angela to call her back as that is putting the "ball into Angela's court." There is a pretty good chance Angela will not call her back anyway and she will be left waiting. Here's what she might say:

> Hi Angela, it's Kathryn O'Brien calling. So sorry I missed you. I was just following up on the email I sent you last week. If you recall, we worked in the same industry several years ago. I have been Director of Public Relations with a major hospital until just recently when I was downsized due to a reorganization in the health care sector. I am hoping to meet with you to ask you a few questions and to get your perspective on opportunities in this market. I will try you back tomorrow. Thanks again.

When Kathryn calls the following day, she may again hit voice mail and should be prepared to leave a similar message. In fact, Kathryn should be ready to call somewhere between five and seven times before she is successful. In later calls – perhaps #4 – she might leave her telephone number by saying, "If it's more convenient for you to call me back, I will leave my telephone number which is 416-123-4567. I will keep trying you back but feel free to call me anytime."

With persistence, Kathryn will eventually connect with Angela. Once they do speak, Kathryn should be ready in case she encounters some resistance to meeting. For example, Angela might throw up blocks such as, "I'm unable to help you," or "I don't have time to meet you." If this happens, Kathryn should at least try to get something of value from the call such as seeking advice on where to go next, asking for a referral, or probing for information.

Conducting the meeting

Let's say Kathryn secures a meeting with Angela. She should be prepared to conduct this session the same she would any other professional meeting. That means being sociable and showing interest in the other person but remaining focused on meeting her objectives.

Kathryn's objectives might vary but will include:

- Obtaining information from Angela about trends – particularly hiring trends – in the industry;
- Discussing how her skills might be transferrable to other industries;
- Brainstorming other career options;
- Identifying key people, ideally decision makers, in other organizations that Kathryn might be able to meet with;
- Obtaining feedback on her resume and job search strategy; and
- Learning about any openings that Angela might know about.

Typically, Kathryn would begin the meeting by thanking Angela for agreeing to meet with her and assuring her that she will take no more than the previously agreed upon time.

Then, she may want to re-introduce her background and bring Angela up to date on what she has been doing over the years, particularly if they haven't had much contact in recent times. Something like, "It's been about ten years since you and I worked together on several projects. Let me bring you up to date on what I've been doing since then. "

At that point, Kathryn will slide smoothly into a clear and brief description of what she has been doing. It makes sense to approach this in a chronological way, starting from when they last worked together.

Although Kathryn may have her resume with her, she should refrain from giving it to Angela at this point as it could distract from the actual conversation. The resume can be brought out later.

As Kathryn wraps up her description of what she has been doing, she should explain what her plans are: "At this stage, I am planning to remain in the public relations sector and I am exploring what those options might be and in what types of industries. And I was hoping that you might be able to provide some feedback to me on how I can do that."

At this point, Angela will likely have some questions for Kathryn or some suggestions. However, Kathryn should come armed with specific questions framed around the information she is trying to obtain. Here are a few examples:

> Does that approach makes sense and what advice would you have for me?
> What do you see as the future trends in your industry?
> What other companies or people might you suggest I contact?
> Might you be willing to give them a call on my behalf and introduce me?
> Is it okay if I mention your name?
> Can you take a look at my resume and offer me some feedback?
> Do you know the names of any recruiters who specialize in my field?
> Do you have any thoughts on how my skills and background might be transferred to other industries or types of jobs?
> Are you aware of any companies in the area with openings in my field?

Having a good list of focused questions will highlight Kathryn's seriousness and professionalism and help her obtain valuable information for her job search.

One final note about this meeting: It is important that Kathryn not ask Angela for a job or if any openings exist in her company. Remember, the purpose of the meeting is fact-finding. Kathryn can assume that if Angela did happen to have openings in her own company that she thought Kathryn might be suited for, she would mention them. Asking Angela directly for a job would be a big turnoff and possibly negate the value of the meeting.

Following up the meeting

Always write a thank you note by mail or email regardless of how helpful the meeting was. Send this note shortly after the meeting – within two to three days

– and make sure they know how much you appreciate their time and the advice they shared. Kathryn could write something like this:

> Angela, thank you so much for taking the time to meet with me yesterday and sharing your insights into my job search strategy. As a result of your suggestions, I have been successful in arranging two meetings, one with a PR agency and another with a not-for-profit agency.
>
> I found your perspectives to be informative. You've got me thinking in a whole new way and I really value the information I left with. Above all, I appreciate your personal support and will keep you posted on the progress of my search.
>
> All the best,
> Kathryn

Note that Kathryn said she would keep Angela informed about her progress. If someone has taken the time to meet with you, they likely have an interest in how you are doing, even after you've obtained a new job. So send them regular updates. It's a great way to stay in touch with a valuable contact.

BEFORE MOVING ON

1. Make sure that you develop your list of personal connections. I think it is best to use a spreadsheet so you can keep an accurate, up-to-date record of who you contacted and when, and what was discussed.

Ask Gerry

Q. I am getting conflicting opinions on whether it is better to communicate with potential employers by telephone or email. What do you think?

A. Most job seekers rely on email as their preferred way of connecting with potential employers. The problem is: it's not very effective. That's because most managers are overwhelmed by emails every day and only have time to respond to the most urgent ones. There are people who have thousands of unread emails in their inbox which means there is a good chance your email will not be read. So, here's what you should do. Drop the idea of using email and pick up the phone. Yes, the good old fashioned phone! Now, I understand that making telephone calls to a

---

potential employer can be one of the most difficult things for any job seeker to do, especially for those of you who are not used to using the phone to sell things.

Think of it this way: the telephone is a great way to establish a personal connection – even if you end up leaving a voice mail – because the person on the other end gets an immediate impression of you from your telephone manner and the tone of your voice. And since most people are afraid of using the phone, the fact that you are doing so demonstrates a degree of confidence that others may not have. This quality will not go unnoticed by the employer.

To make the most of your call, be sure to do at least some basic research about the company including figuring out what its key challenges and issues are. Then, without sounding too scripted, write down the key points you want to make in the order you want to make them. And always prepare a good opening that should include something like, "Is this a convenient time to speak?"

Try to find a location for the call that is private, quiet and free from distracting background noises. Screeching kids, music or traffic will come across as unprofessional. And give thought to which type of phone you use. Usually, a landline has better call quality than a mobile phone but that is not always the case if you use a cordless phone, especially when used with a head set.

Lastly, maintain a record of all the calls you make. This will include the date, who you spoke to, a summary of what was said, and your next step. You don't want to overlook a key follow-up date or activity. And always follow-up the call with an email (yes – an email is fine here!) thanking the person for their time.

Chapter 16

Connecting With Employers Directly

"When one door closes, another opens; but we often look so long and so regretfully upon the closed door that we do not see the one which has opened for us."

– Alexander Graham Bell

TARGETING SPECIFIC ORGANIZATIONS that you feel you might want to work for is one of the most valuable steps in your job search. Ideally, you will have a personal connection, someone who can "open the door" for you but if you simply cannot find anyone to give you a referral, you will have to take it upon yourself to make that contact.

Your goal in approaching companies directly is to obtain a meeting – ideally in person – to introduce yourself, learn about specific careers, and generally network with the person you are meeting to uncover possible job opportunities. In job search vernacular, this meeting is known as the "informational interview."

An informational interview is an effective way for you to get information without having a formal interview scheduled. Essentially what you are doing is identifying a company you are interested in, or an individual who is in a field you'd like to learn about, and asking them if they are willing to meet and share their advice with you.

There are two types of informational interviews and it is important to understand the distinction. One type is an informational interview obtained because someone else has recommended you. This is very generous on the part of both parties (the referrer and the company they've contacted) but let's face it – the interviewer is doing you a favour. There is little benefit to the interviewer. In this instance, you can probably relax a little bit and not worry as much about impressing them. But still come prepared with a good set of questions and a plan to gain good intelligence that will help your job search elsewhere.

The second type of informational interview is one you have obtained on your own. This is a completely different story because the interviewer most likely has her own agenda for meeting with you. Most employers don't do these meetings out of the goodness of their heart. They usually have a reason. It could be that they are looking for someone now or might be down the road. Whatever the reason, this interview needs to be taken seriously and treated like a regular interview.

Here are the steps you should follow to open doors for you:

Step 1 – Set a target list

You first have to develop a target list of industries and organizations you are interested in and might like to work for. For example, you might have an interest in manufacturing, health care, professional services, government or not-for-profit. Once you know the sectors that hold some interest for you, you can start to identify organizations within that sector.

Many people believe that the largest employers have the most jobs, and while that may be true, many are also going through consolidation and downsizing to control costs and may not be adding staff. So, don't overlook the small to mid-sized employers in your chosen sectors. Although these companies are not as well-known, they can be a much better source of employment for you – primarily because most other people will overlook them.

How do you find the names of these organizations?

There are many online business directories that will give you good leads about companies to contact. You should start with the membership list of your local chamber of commerce or board of trade. Virtually every employer of consequence is a member of the chamber or board. In many cases, these directories are available free online. If they are not and you have to be a member to access the list, most chambers offer an individual membership at a very low cost. Joining up would be a very worthwhile investment for you.

In doing the research for this book, I took a quick look at the various chambers across Canada. Those who offer free access to their membership directories include: Calgary Chamber of Commerce, Regina and District Chamber of Commerce, Winnipeg Chamber of Commerce, Ottawa Chamber of Commerce, Toronto Board of Trade and Halifax Chamber of Commerce. The Board of

Trade of Metropolitan Montreal allows partial access and the Vancouver Board of Trade requires that you be a member to access the information.

There are also numerous "lists" of companies that you can review to come up with ideas and contact information. Here are a few that might help you:

- Best Workplaces in Canada – Great Place to Work
- Canada's Best Employers: The Top 50 – Canadian Business
- Best Small and Medium Employers
- Canada's Top 100 Employers
- Top 50 Socially Responsible Companies – Maclean's
- Canada's 50 Best Managed Companies
- Canada's Fastest Growing Companies – Profit Guide

Many of these lists contain basic information about the companies, like names of key contact people and descriptions of their products and services. And with a few clicks, you can be on their website where you will find all other information you need to know to make an informed approach.

Step 2 - Research

Once you have prepared a ranking of the companies you'd like to contact, you should start to research them to develop a better understanding of the key issues and challenges facing them. You need to know this information so you can customize your letter and also to prepare you for the face-to-face meeting you are hoping to have. It also demonstrates that you have taken the time to prepare, something most other people don't bother doing.

As a guideline, most employer's challenges fall into one or more of these categories:

- Growing their revenue
- Decreasing expenses
- Expanding into new markets, products or services
- Battling their competitors
- Strengthening their financial management
- Dealing with human resource issues
- Building relationships with stakeholders

Ask yourself this question: Is there any way my skills, experience and qualifications can help my target company deal with these challenges?

In addition to knowing about the company, you'll need to research the individual you are sending the letter to and whom you hope to meet. You can do this easily through LinkedIn, or if they're not on LinkedIn, just Google them to find out if you have any interests or background in common with them.

Step 3 - Communicate

The actual steps involved in contacting companies directly are almost the same as those you would use when contacting your personal connections. Except in this case, you are contacting people who could possibly hire you. When contacting your personal connections, you are mostly seeking advice from them.

I would always recommend that you personalize and direct your letter to the appropriate hiring manager – not the human resource department. For example, if you are an accountant, you should send your letter to the controller or chief financial officer. If you are a programmer, you should send your letter to the information technology manager. (Of course, if you are looking for a job in human resources, you would send your letter to the HR department – but that's the only time.)

The reason for taking this approach is that the hiring manager will be aware of the company's staffing needs before the HR department and will have a much better handle on their requirements.

And, don't forget, the names of most of these people can be found using LinkedIn. There is some debate about whether or not to include your resume with the marketing letter. Some believe you should give it all you've got and send the resume. Others think the letter should be used to pique the interest of the hiring manager and should be written well enough to entice him to invite you in for a meeting.

I tend to favour the no-resume approach but you might want to try both and see how it goes before deciding on a final strategy.

Unlike the email you would have sent to your personal connections reminding them who you are and asking to meet, your letter to prospective companies should target their needs.

Here is a framework you might use:

Paragraph 1:
Your opening paragraph should be an attention-grabber, stating an industry-wide or organizational problem you can solve.

> With increasing overhead costs and rising expenses, one objective of every organization is to reduce expenses and implement cost-avoidance programs. A key area where gains can be made is health and safety: reducing injuries, achieving fewer lost productivity days and reducing workers' compensation premiums.

Paragraph 2:
State your reason for writing.

> I am writing to determine whether your organization needs someone with my training, experience and education.

Paragraph 3:
List three to five accomplishments that show why you can solve their problems.

> As a certified safety professional, I have made consistent contributions to productivity and profitability. Specifically, I have:
>
> - Managed workers' compensation, loss control, industrial hygiene, medical services, employee assistance and fire prevention functions;
> - Reduced accident claims by 50% through creation of new safety procedures;
> - Organized and trained teams of personnel to implement safety goals and meet objectives of employees, union representatives and management;
> - Reduced potential claims by designing innovative safety programs.

Paragraph 4:
Make a strong closing statement and indicate when you will be following up.

> I would like to discuss how my experience and qualifications could contribute to your organization. I will telephone you in a few days to arrange a mutually convenient appointment.
>
> Sincerely,
>
>
> Your name

Here's a twist: You should think about mailing or hand-delivering your letter, not emailing it. Almost no one sends mail anymore – which is why you should do so. Do the opposite of what everyone else does. You will stand out.

You should follow-up with your contact about five to seven days after mailing your letter. This will allow enough time for the letter to be delivered and read by the hiring manager. If you wait too long, your name and letter will no longer be fresh in their minds.

Your follow-up should also take a route almost no one else takes – a telephone call! What you will say and how you say it is important and requires pre-planning, and lots of practice, before making it.

One thing is certain – you have to speak with an air of confidence and without hesitation or regret. Practising your call technique will help with this.

This script will have to be your own and should sound natural. If the person you are trying to reach doesn't pick up and your call goes to voice mail, be prepared to leave a concise 20 – 30 second speech that says who you are and why you are interested in meeting with them. This would be like an abbreviated version of your elevator speech. You want to quickly recap your background and why you are interested in their company. You should also add that you realize there might not be a job available now and that you would still like to meet with them for a few minutes, if they have time.

End the call by saying that you will call them back in a day or two. Never ask them to call you back as that will put the ball in their court. It is unlikely they will return your call.

One final thing that you have to anticipate is that a large number of these employers will refuse to meet you. No worries – rejection is part of the sales process. While this may be hard on your ego initially, you will start to develop a thicker skin and eventually you will not take this rejection personally. And remember: job searching is a numbers game. The more people you call, the more interviews you will get.

Step 4 – The meeting

Let's say you are successful in getting the meeting. What should you talk about in the meeting?

First, remember that you have already pre-qualified this company as one you think you might like to work for. This means your goal with the informational interview is to learn more about the company and its challenges, uncovered any opportunities that might exist now or in the near future, and link your background and skill set to their needs.

If no opportunities exist right now, you shouldn't be totally disappointed because the meeting itself will have given you a chance to make a positive impression on the hiring manager which will increase the likelihood of her remembering you when a real opportunity arises.

One of the key ingredients of a successful information interview is to have a game plan going in. Like a "real" interview, you should be prepared to engage in small talk at the beginning of the meeting. But unlike a real interview, once that small talk is over, it's your game. You've requested the meeting so you should take charge. The employer you are meeting won't usually have a set of interview questions for you because (theoretically) there's no job available.

Your best bet is to focus your initial questions on the interviewer. Ask about their background and experience, how they got into their present job, and what other careers they considered. Without going on too long, you might ask what they like and dislike about their current job and the company they work for. Generally, people like to talk about themselves so this conversation should be fairly easy. But try to limit it to just a few minutes.

Following this opening, a very useful question to ask is, What are the key issues and challenges facing your business?" This should launch the employer into a description of the things that keep her awake at night. Presumably, if you have done your research well, you already know about most of the issues and challenges they face so it becomes the launch point for you. This is where you can begin to link your skills to their problems. Since this is not a real interview, you can't be too overt about this but you should speak about times when you might have faced and helped solve the same types of problems.

Throughout the entire discussion, your primary goal is to obtain information and advice, not a job, from that employer. As tempting as it might be, you should refrain from asking for a job or asking if there are any openings coming up. That could be a big turnoff to someone who has agreed to spend time with you and help you. In fact, being too direct and asking for a job could put people on the spot and ultimately hurt your chances if a job does arise down the road.

However, if the employer raises the issue first and asks if you might be interested in a role there, by all means, engage in that discussion – as long as it's their idea, not yours.

An informational interview should take about thirty minutes or so. Be respectful of the employer's time and don't overstay your welcome. At the end of the meeting – assuming it has gone well – you should ask the employer if there is anyone else they would recommend you meet. Keep in mind that when they refer you to someone, they are putting their reputation on the line.

Ask Gerry

Q. I have been out of work for a couple of months and am considering taking a part-time contract while continuing to look for full time work. Is this a good idea?

A. If your eventual goal is to find a full-time job, it is possible that a part-time contract will distract you from that goal. So, be careful. By now you should have laid the groundwork for your search and you should have a well-oiled system set up and running to connect with possible opportunities. If, for example, you accept a three-month contract that requires your full-time attention (40 hours a week), you risk jeopardizing all the work you have done and the relationships you have built so far. However, if the contract requires only 10 or 20 hours a week, or if it is full-time but only for a few weeks, then you might want to consider accepting it. Not only will you earn a little money but you might build new skills and meet new people that could lead to a full-time job.

Following the meeting, you must follow up with a thank you note. Regardless of how helpful the information was, you have to show your appreciation for their time. It is also wise to keep that person in the loop by e-mailing them after you've met with one of their referrals or after you've gotten a job. It will certainly make them feel good if some of the advice they shared has paid off.

If you make a good impression in an informational interview, it could ultimately lead to a job. This meeting differs from those you have with your personal connections because you're not there just to ask for advice. You are there to convince them to feel comfortable hiring you directly or referring you to someone else who could hire you.

So even if an informational interview doesn't lead directly to a job, it could lead to another informational interview that could lead to a job. The more informational interviews you have, the better chance you have of landing the job you want.

Keeping track of your calls

In the course of your job search, you will connect with many people and it is impossible for you to keep track of everything in your head. That's why it is important to maintain a log of your calls – that you review daily – so that you stay organized and avoid missed opportunities. Here is a sample log sheet that you might use to track all your activity.

LOG SHEET

Company name	JS Machinery and Equipment
Contact person	John Smith
Telephone #	(604) 222-222
Date letter mailed	Feb 2nd
Phone call #1	Feb 9th – left VM
Phone call #2	Feb 11th – left VM
Phone call #3	
Phone call #4	
Tel conversation held	Feb 12th
Did I get meeting?	Yes
Meeting date	Feb 25th
Thank you note sent	Feb 27th
Notes	Mr. Smith said they may be doing some hiring in late March and to check back then. He gave me three referrals to contact
Next follow-up	Mar 25th

BEFORE MOVING ON

1. Complete your research and develop a list of those organizations you would like to speak to. Then prepare scripts and a strategy for connecting with them.

Chapter 17

Establish Relationships
With Recruiters

"Never tell me the sky's the limit when there are
footprints on the moon."

–Author Unknown

LET ME START by saying that the terms executive search firms, executive recruiters, employment agencies, placement firms, and head-hunters all mean the same thing – they work for *employers* to source and screen candidates for job openings.

Now, here's the problem. Some of you will believe (mistakenly) that a recruitment firm will find you a job. That is wrong, and you shouldn't be misled into thinking that a recruiter is working for you. While you may have a good professional relationship with one or more recruiters, you must remember their primary obligation is to their client – the employer – who has hired them. You will only be recommended to one of their clients if the recruiter believes you have the necessary background and qualifications their client is seeking.

Having said all that, even if it means lowering your expectations, it is in your best interest to be on the radar of recruiters who regularly fill positions in your field.

Why is this?

Recruiters are often aware of positions that need to be filled right away. For example, if an employer (client) has a sudden vacancy caused by a dismissal, an employee quitting without notice, or becoming ill and not able to work anymore, they might need to find a replacement immediately. They may not be interested in conducting a full search to find the absolute best candidate for the job. Instead, they might be happy to find someone who meets many of the qualifications (but not all) and most importantly, is available right away. If they ask a recruiter to recommend candidates and you are "top of mind" with that recruiter, you have a good chance of being referred by the recruiter.

Types of recruiters

Remember, recruiters are paid by the employer, the hiring company. They are usually grouped by how they are paid.

"Retained" recruiters are retained by the company and paid their full fee regardless of the outcome of the search. This means that if the company calls off the search for some reason or simply decides not to hire anyone, the recruiter still gets paid for conducting the search process.

In most cases, the full fee – whether it is a pre-determined fixed amount or a percent of salary – is paid one-third at the beginning of the search, one-third upon presentation of candidates, and one-third upon conclusion.

"Contingency" recruiters are paid only if a candidate they recommend is hired by the employer. Their fee is contingent upon a placement. If someone is hired, they get paid. In the previous example I gave, where the employer called off the search, no fee would be payable to the recruiter.

But the differences are more significant than just how the recruiter is paid. It has a great deal with how the work is carried out, and what results the employer can expect.

Contingency firms are generally used for junior-to-middle level positions, where many people are likely to be qualified for the position. The salary levels for these positions are usually under $75,000 however some contingency firms place individuals in positions over $100,000.

Contingency firms – since they have no guarantee of being paid – cannot afford to invest a large amount of time and resources on any one search simply because the outcome may depend on several factors beyond the recruiter's control. The candidate sourcing activities of contingency firms tend to be limited to their own internal database of candidates, postings on various job boards and their own website, and social media. Speed is of the essence. Their goal is to find candidate matches and send the resumes of these candidates to the employer as quickly as possible.

Because their sourcing activities are limited, contingency firms want to present "good" candidates but they cannot be certain they are the "best possible" candidates. This is because they will not have conducted an exhaustive search of the market.

Many times a contingency recruiter does not have an exclusive arrangement with the employer, meaning that the employer may be using more than one recruiting firm. It is important for you to know this, especially if you have relationships with more than one firm. (It would be awkward if more than one firm presented you as a candidate.)

Retained recruiters are used to fill middle-to-senior level positions where finding the best possible candidates is important. And since they are paid to complete a process and are paid regardless of the outcome, the activities of retained recruiters will differ in certain respects from contingency recruiters.

First, retained recruiters will conduct a detailed, original search to identify qualified individuals who may not be aware of the job opening but who might be interested in applying. In accomplishing this task, the recruiter will identify targeted organizations and individuals within those organizations who might be prospective candidates. It is possible this list will include people who work for competitors of the client.

This is an example when being visible on social media could work to your advantage. If you are active and seen as being a thought leader, your visibility will increase and the probability of being noticed by the recruiter during the research phase increases.

Second, a retained firm will likely be working exclusively on the search and they are expected to evaluate all candidates, internal and external, being considered for the position. As a result, a retained firm should not present a candidate to more than one employer at a time.

Lastly, a retained firm (because they are being paid for the process) will often conduct many other activities to ensure the candidate hired is the best available candidate. This list could include:

- Completing detailed reference checks
- Administering personality assessments
- Verifying academic credentials
- Conducting criminal and credit background checks
- Attending candidate interviews with the client

- Facilitating the selection process
- Preparing and negotiating the final job offer

Ask Gerry

Q. I am happy where I am but every once in a while, an executive recruiter will contact me about a job opportunity. I am wondering if you could provide a couple of quick tips on how to handle this situation? Is it professional to speak with recruiters when they call?

A. Even though you are happily employed, I see no harm in "keeping your eyes open" for good opportunities that could possibly advance your career. That's just good career management. It is also wise to maintain relationships with recruiters in your field, although you better not mislead them by implying that you are looking for another job when you really are not. They will be quite happy if you inform them you are not actively searching but to keep sending you notices of jobs so you can keep abreast of what's going on. After all, you never know when circumstances might change with your current employer.

Tips to build a relationship with a recruiter

1. You should treat your relationship with a recruiter professionally – the same way you would with any employer. You should think of every interaction as you would an interview. Even though the recruiter does not have the final hiring authority, if you don't get past the recruiter you will never get to meet the employer.

2. Always be helpful to the recruiter. If one calls about an opportunity that you decide to decline, try to recommend someone else who might be a better fit.

3. Be selective in the firms you choose to work with. Research directories and websites carefully to determine which firms regularly place candidates in your field. If a firm never has a search for the type of job you are looking for, you will only be wasting your time and theirs by contacting them.

4. Don't give any firm the exclusive right to work on your behalf and steer clear of any firm that wants a fee from you to "find" you a job.

5. Be specific about the type of job you are seeking and what your expected salary expectations are. This will save everyone a lot of time. If you are interested in an opportunity presented to you by a recruiter but later change your mind, let the recruiter know as quickly as possible. If you delay and withdraw at the last minute after an interview with the employer is already set up – it will be embarrassing to the recruiter and will likely be the last time he or she presents an opportunity to you.

6. Do not expect the recruiter to prepare your resume for you. If you need outside help, ask someone else to do it. However the recruiter might have ideas on how to improve your resume and you should heed the advice.

8. Strive for a face-to-face meeting with the recruiter but understand that he or she will probably only want to meet with you if there is a good probability of a job vacancy in your area of expertise in the near future. Otherwise, you will be asked to submit your resume online or by email.

9. Stay in touch periodically with the recruiter so that you maintain that top of mind awareness. You do this not by calling and asking, "Have you found anything for me yet?" Instead, you should refer possible leads about upcoming job vacancies to them; comment on any online posts they make; and every so often send an email saying that you're still pursuing good job opportunities.

One final reminder: in your correspondence with a recruiter, be clear that you do not want your resume sent to any employer without your prior consent. This is necessary to prevent an unscrupulous recruiter from sending your resume, unsolicited, to several companies in the hope of collecting a placement fee should one of these employers hire you sometime in the future. This doesn't occur often but it is worth noting.

BEFORE MOVING ON

1. Make a list of the recruiters in your area. Carefully review their websites to make sure they are currently working on (or have worked on) searches in your field. Figure out which recruiter would be the best one to connect with and try to make an appointment with him or her.

Chapter 18

Responding to Publicized
Job Openings

"It is never too late to be what you might have been."

- George Eliot

AS YOU KNOW by now, job openings that are publicized on job boards, on company websites, in newspapers or trade journals account for at most 20% of total job openings. And since most job seekers take the easy way, most spend all their efforts applying to publicized openings. This means that for every published opening, there will be hundreds of applicants – guaranteed! Which lowers the probability this route will work well for you. That's why I suggest that you only spend 20% of your job search time here.

Here are seven tips to make the most efficient use of your time applying to publicized job openings:

Tip #1: Think about whether the job already has been filled

Take a look at the job posting date and the application deadline. If a job is posted January 15th and the closing date for applications is January 22nd, you can pretty much assume the company already has someone in mind, usually an internal candidate, for the job. These hiring managers are simply trying to justify to their superiors that they've considered other candidates when in fact they've already made their mind up. Governments – for some reason – seem to be guilty of this action. Applying in situations like this is probably a waste of your time.

Tip #2: Be creative when answering sticky questions

When completing online applications, which require every field to be filled out, you should be creative when asked about items that are best left to later in the interview process. For example, if the online form asks you to state your salary history, you should insert $1 or $10, or any number to show you're not about to reveal your salary history until you've learned more about the job you are applying for.

Likewise, if the form asks for references, you should insert "Relevant references provided at a later date." The rule is that references should only be provided after you have met with the employer and concluded this is an opportunity to want to pursue. If your skills closely match the employer's requirements, not answering questions exactly as asked will not rule you out.

A last piece of advice: if the online form requires you to list your work experience in a field, do all the editing first in a Word doc (or similar program) where it is easier to pick up typos and other mistakes. Once you are satisfied with the final product, cut and paste it into the form. This will help ensure your written comments are clear, concise and free of typos and grammatical or spelling errors.

Tip #3: Use keywords intelligently

In completing an online application, or even if you are sending a resume as an email attachment, you should insert keywords that appear in the job posting or job description. Many larger organizations and most recruiting firms use applicant tracking systems that do more than "track" candidates. They are often used to filter applications automatically based on selected criteria such as keywords, skills, former employers, years of experience and schools attended.

Think carefully about how you incorporate keywords into your cover letter and resume. Some people choose to use them within the body of the cover letter and resume, while others simply list them at the bottom of the resume.

Even if your resume is being reviewed the old-fashioned way by someone actually reading it, using keywords and phrases will increase your chance of being selected for an interview.

For example, a candidate applying for a Communications Advisor position might use the following resume keywords: *writing, social media, communications, public relations, employee communications, media relations, and marketing.*

It's important to think beyond the actual job you are applying for. That's because if you don't get the job, your resume will remain in the applicant tracking system of the company. A manager in another department might be searching the database for an opening he has and will use keywords and phrases to search for candidates. If you've planned well, your resume might pop up in his search.

Tip #4: Use your personal connections even when applying online

As we showed earlier in this chapter, you have a lengthy list of personal connections. And they too have lengthy lists. So when applying to an online posting where you know no one at the company, ask your personal connections if they happen to know anyone at the company and would they be willing to give you a warm introduction. You can be certain that if a senior manager asks the HR department to "keep an eye open" for a resume from you, your submission will be given more attention than if nothing was said.

Likewise, if you do happen to have a good contact at the company, you might consider contacting that person directly with a cover letter and resume and bypass the online process. If you do take that route, follow up a few days later with a call or email to make sure your information was received.

Tip #5: Sending your resume as an email attachment

If the posting instructs you to send your cover letter and resume as an email attachment, there are a few rules of thumb you should use:

- Save your documents as PDF documents to protect the format. They will then arrive in the same format as you sent them.

- Name your documents so they make sense to the recipient. Use:

  Cover letter – Your Name
  Resume – Your Name

- Write a brief email cover letter of no more than one or two short paragraphs that explains what you are applying for and directs the reader to the attached cover letter and resume.

- Make sure the Subject line clearly explains who you are and what job you are applying for. Use something like:

  Application for Communications Advisor – Your Name
  Job #123: Project Accountant – Your Name

- Make sure the contact information on your email signature is the same as the information on your resume. Quite often, people email their resume from their work email, which has work contact information in the signature. This implies that it is okay to contact you at work, which may not be what you want.

- It's always a good habit to send a copy of your email submission to yourself for your own records. To do so, simply bcc yourself.

Tip #6: Wait a few days before applying

Whether you are applying by filling out an online application or sending in your resume as an email attachment, you should wait a few days before replying. Why? What usually happens is that a large number of people respond the first day a job is posted. On the receiving end (where I am) it is natural to conclude that most, if not all, of these applicants have put absolutely no time into preparing their application. They have made no effort to determine if their skills and qualifications match the requirements we are seeking. As a result, the seriousness of their application tends to be lessened. You don't want to be thought of that way.

But perhaps the more important reason for waiting a few days before applying is that you want your resume to be near the top of the pile. After the first two or three days of a posting, the flow of new resumes will start to decline. If the employer prints off the resumes, the last ones received will be on top of the pile. If she leaves them in her email inbox, the last ones received will be near the top of her inbox.

Tip #7: Make sure you are a good fit

This tip may seem obvious but the more specific your skills and background match the requirements listed in the ad, the greater the chance you have of being selected for an interview. If you believe you are a close fit, obtain as much information about the company as possible before responding; then customize your cover letter to show how you closely match the company's needs. If you do this well, you will stand out from other applicants.

A final point: Please don't forget that applying for jobs online is the easiest way to look for work. Unfortunately it is also the *least effective way*. Don't be like many people who spend 100% of their job search efforts applying online only to be left wondering why they've had no success. Despite the thousands of job boards out there promising an easy route to employment, your best opportunities will still come from people you know.

How to Use Job Boards Effectively

There are literally hundreds and hundreds of online job boards available for Canadian jobs. And trying to navigate your way through this maze can be confusing if you are new to the job search process. Here are a few guidelines for using these job boards and suggestions on how to be more effective at it.

For professional positions. In Canada, most of the professions (accounting, law, engineering, architecture, planning, health care, human resources, finance, and many others) are regulated provincially which means there are provincial bodies with an "umbrella" national organization. Depending of the particular profession, job openings may be posted on the provincial website or the national website. From your perspective, the best way to approach this is to simply google your profession plus the name of the province you want to work in.

For example, if you google "human resources Alberta," the governing body Human Resources Institute of Alberta should be within the first few search results. Likewise, "urban planner Ontario" will quickly get you to the site of the Ontario Professional Planners Institute.

You should also check the websites of the corresponding national bodies as employers may choose to advertise there instead. You would take the same approach. For example, googling for "accounting Canada" will bring you to CPA Canada (Chartered Professional Accountants Canada.)

General job boards. General job boards provide postings of almost every type of job out there. These include jobs in administration, customer service, sales, hospitality, food and beverage, information technology, trades, manufacturing, retail, logistics, government, health care, not-for-profit, and many more. Some of the more popular general job boards include:

CareerBuilder (careerbuilder.ca)
Workopolis (workopolis.ca)
Monster Canada (monster.ca)
Career Beacon (careerbeacon.com)

Even sites such as Craigslist (craiglist.ca) and Kijiji (kijiji.ca), which we typically think of as sites for online classified advertisements, have large sections devoted to job postings.

Industry-specific sites. Some employers will advertise on sites that are specific to their industry regardless of the occupational area. Among these sites are:

Not-for-profit (charityvillage.com)
Municipal government (municipalworld.com)
Oil and gas (careersinoilandgas.com)
Information technology (cips.ca)
Technology (dice.com)

Aggregators. Perhaps the most popular sites are ones that gather (or aggregate) job postings that are listed elsewhere. These include:

Eluta (eluta.ca)
Job Bank (jobbank.gc.ca)
Indeed (ca.indeed.com)
Canada Jobs (canadajobs.com)
Simply Hired (simplyhired.ca)
Hot Jobs (hotjobscanada.ca)

A word of caution: you can easily become overwhelmed by these job boards and spend a disproportionate amount of time on them. For most, you can set up alerts or notifiers which will let you know when a new job in your field is posted. Manage your time wisely on these sites. Remember, they only account for 20% of available jobs.

Newspapers. Admittedly, fewer and fewer organizations are advertising their job openings in the newspaper but you should keep an eye on your local paper nevertheless. The organizations that tend to still use newspapers are those who feel they have an obligation to notify the public of what they are doing, such as governments, NGOs and certain not-for-profits.

Section Four

The Interview

"Job interviews are like first dates. Good impressions count. Awkwardness can occur. Outcomes are unpredictable"

- Unknown

Chapter 19

What to Expect in an Interview

**"Talent will get you in the door
but character will keep you in the room."**

- Unknown

WHEN SEARCHING FOR a new position, you may encounter a variety of interview formats ranging from completely unstructured interviews, which end up being casual conversations over coffee, to highly-structured ones, where the interviewer asks pre-planned questions in an organized way. For some candidates, the latter style feels like an interrogation, direct and unfriendly. Others crave structure and feel uncomfortable when interviews are informal and loose. In my experience, most interviews fall somewhere between those extremes.

One simple way to reduce the ambiguity surrounding the format is to just ask what form the interview will take. When an employer calls or emails you to book an appointment, it's perfectly acceptable to ask about the format of the interview. The person booking the meeting may not know the answer to that question, but you should at least make the effort to find out.

You should also find out the name and title of the person (or people) you will be meeting and the expected length of the interview. The best way to find out is to ask the person who invited you. You don't want to go into an interview thinking you're meeting the HR person for a brief screening interview only to discover that you're actually being interviewed by a panel of five people including the CEO. That has happened. How awkward!

Regardless of the format, the interviewer will be trying to answer the following questions while you're sitting before them:

Question 1. Do you have the necessary skills to do the job?

To help them answer this query, gather as much background information on the company as you can so that you can explain how your skills match their needs. After studying the job description, research the organization's strategic plan and media releases. Even speak to people you know who work there, or people who do business with the organization.

Question 2. Are you the right fit with our organization?

Fit is one of the great intangibles and is a lot harder to measure than specific skills. Interviewers often rely on their gut feelings (or intuition) to determine whether or not someone is a good fit for a job and organization. It's not a perfect science, I know. But that's how most employers approach this question. And unfortunately it is also how a lot of skilled and qualified people get passed over for jobs.

The chemistry between you and the interviewer also plays an important role in determining fit. If the interviewer doesn't get a good feeling about you, even if you have good skills, you won't get beyond the first interview.

Question 3. Will you do what it takes to help us meet our goals and solve our problems?

Remember, the needs of most companies fall into these categories:

- Increasing revenue
- Decreasing expenses
- Solving specific problems
- Building relationships with customers and stakeholders
- Strengthening financial management
- Improving human resource practices
- Developing new initiatives and ideas

You can be guaranteed the interviewer will be trying to determine whether or not you can help them tackle current and future needs.

Types of Interviews

Essentially, there are four types of interviews:

Screening interviews. These interviews are usually conducted by the human resources department to determine if you have the minimum skills and experience to do the job. They may also try to measure fit with some form of personality testing. In most cases, the HR person will not have deep knowledge of the job and may not be able to answer specific questions that you may have about the role. But don't underestimate the importance of screening interviews. If you "pass" this stage, you will be screened into the next round of interviews.

Immediate supervisor interview. The person asking the questions in an immediate supervisor interview is your potential boss and they usually have final hiring authority. In those situations, you can expect to talk specifics, so come prepared to explain how you will solve their problems. The interviewer will also be trying to determine how well you will work with him and the team.

Co-worker interview. Depending on the culture of the organization, you may be asked to meet with some potential co-workers. This is usually a good sign, as it signals that the organization seeks advice from staff and values their input. When being interviewed by potential co-workers, provide a short overview of your background and emphasize your desire to join and contribute to their team. While co-workers are not decision-makers, they can influence the hiring decisions that organizations make.

Panel interview. An employer may also take a "panel" approach to interviewing. To get various opinions, they might invite representatives from several departments to participate in the process. While this can be daunting for some candidates, as all eyes are on you, remember to speak to every member of the panel when answering questions. Some individuals make the mistake of only speaking to the person who asks the question, or the most senior person in the room. Also scan the room, make eye contact with all panel members and shake hands with everyone at the beginning and at the end of the interview.

The Flow of an Interview

Regardless of the type of interview (screening, supervisor, panel, etc.), most structured interviews adhere to the following format:

Step 1 – Greeting and icebreaker

The greeting is where the interviewer gets that all-important first impression of you. Whether it is your handshake, eye contact, smile, appearance, or demeanor, impressions of you will start to form right away. There will also be some pleasant small talk (called the "icebreaker") as you are introduced and seated. Some people excel at this part of the interview; others do not. An experienced interviewer will try to put you at ease by talking about the weather, a sports game, or whether the traffic was bad getting to the interview. Usually pretty mundane topics. If the interviewer doesn't initiate some small talk, you should take over. But keep your comments brief and respond when the interviewer signals that it's time to begin the main part of the interview.

Ask Gerry

Q. Is it really necessary to research the company and the people I will be meeting before going to the interview?

A. Yes, yes, yes! These days, it is so easy to access company information online that it's inexcusable for you to enter an interview uninformed about the company, their industry, their competitors and the challenges they are facing.

Likewise, you can gain lots of good information about the people you will be meeting through the company's website, LinkedIn, Facebook, Twitter and other web sources. Anything interesting you find, like their hobbies or interests, should be casually mentioned during the interview to illustrate that you've taken the time to do the research.

Step 2 – Opening (introduction)

In most cases, the interviewer will open by telling you what the agenda is for the interview. She will reference the planned format and state the approximate length of the interview. The dialogue might go something like this:

> Thank you very much for joining us. We are going to take about 45 minutes to learn about your education, background and skills. We have a series of questions we'd like to go through with you. After those questions, you will have a chance to ask questions of us. Is that okay?

Step 3 – The tell-me-about-yourself question

Nine times out of ten, the opening question will be a biographical one. This is what I usually say when I interview candidates: "To start us off, would you mind taking a few minutes to introduce yourself? Why don't you start with your education first and then tell me about your work history, from oldest to most recent?" Regardless of how the opening question is asked, you should take five to ten minutes to communicate your background. In doing so, you should pay special attention to those areas of your work history that you feel are particularly relevant to the job you're being interviewed for.

Step 4 – Employer asks targeted questions

After you finish answering the tell-me-about-yourself question, the interviewer will probably have some specific questions for you.

The absolute best way to prepare for an interview is to anticipate the questions you are going to be asked. The most effective way to do that is to engage in some quick role reversal. Pretend that you're the interviewer. What questions would *you* ask candidates to determine if they have the necessary skills and experience for the job?

Also use the job ad or job description, if you have it, to complete this task. If you do this properly, you will be able to reasonably predict about 80% of the questions that you will face in an interview. If you do your homework, the interview will seem like an open-book exam!

To give you a hand with this task, there's a list of the most commonly-asked interview questions in Chapter 21. Remember that questions are structured in one of three ways:

Close-ended (which require short, sometimes one-word, answers)
- Did you major in accounting?
- What was your salary in your last job?
- Who did you report do?

Open-ended (requiring a more descriptive answer)
- Tell me about your educational background?
- How do you like managing a large staff?
- Why did you leave your last job?

Behavioral (looking for a past example)
- Tell me of a time when you had to deal with a very irate customer. What was the problem? What actions did you take? How was it resolved?

Regardless of how questions are posed, your answers should focus on how you can add value to the employer, not what the employer can do for you.

Step 5 – You are given an opportunity to ask questions

Near the end of the interview, the interviewer will probably ask if you have any questions that you would like to ask of them. Having no questions sends the message that you are not interested in the job or have not bothered to prepare. Remember, the questions you ask must be insightful and focus on the job, the people and the organization.

Step 6 – The close

Watch for signals that it is time to bring the interview to a close. After you find out what the next steps are, express your thanks to the interviewer for her time, affirm your interest in the job and your desire to move things forward, and shake everyone's hand. In the same way that you tried to make a strong first impression when you entered the room, focus on leaving a positive impression as you exit. You want to exude confidence and trust. A weak ending could negate a strong interview.

What to Bring to an Interview

I must say, I can be really put off by candidates who come to an interview with nothing in their hands. What it says to me is that the individual has not bothered to prepare for the interview, otherwise they would have brought some kind of briefing notes. It also tells me they are probably disorganized as they have no method of taking notes or jotting down reminders from the interviewers.

After interviewing more than 10,000 candidates over 25+ years as an executive recruiter, here is my checklist of what you should bring to an interview:

Directions. If you're not absolutely sure where you're going and how to get there, then bring directions with you. You should also allow plenty of time to get to your interview.

Cell phone. Bring your mobile phone and the contact information of the person that you're meeting in case you're delayed by unexpected circumstances. However, please leave your mobile device in your car or turn it off before entering the interview. Nothing is more disrespectful than a phone going off during an interview.

Identification. You may be asked to show ID at a security desk before entering the building, so bring a piece of photo ID with you.

Professional-looking notebook. Note taking is a very important part of any meeting, including interviews, as it conveys that you want to remember important items from the meeting. Also make a point of asking if it's okay to take a few notes, before you start doing so.

Pens or pencils. Come armed with a handful of pens or pencils, in case one runs out of ink or lead.

Extra copies of your resume. Even if you submitted a resume with your original application, it's smart to bring additional copies in case the interviewer has misplaced her copy, or if others join in the interview and don't have your resume. It is also helpful to do this if you have updated your resume, since you first submitted it. It (almost) goes without saying that your resume must be on high quality paper and the print quality must be crisp.

List of references. Also bring your list of professional references with you. Be sure to include names, titles, the person's connection to you (ex. former boss) as well as their contact information (email and phone). If it seems the employer will be contacting them, you should notify your references immediately, and fill them in on the job details so that they can be prepared for any inquiries after an interview.

List of questions to ask. Bringing a short list of questions with you also demonstrates that you have spent time preparing for the interview (see Chapters 4 and 5 for more information on questions).

Names of the people you are meeting. While this may seem obvious, many people arrive at interviews not knowing the name or names of the people that they are meeting. Being able to address someone by their name, especially someone you've just met, is very impressive.

Sample of your work. For certain jobs, especially creative ones like graphic artists, it is helpful to demonstrate your work by showing examples of what you have done in the past.

Personal items. Finally, it is always good to plan ahead. So bring your reading glasses (if you need them), a hair brush (in case it's windy), an umbrella (if it's raining) and even a shoe cloth to give your shoes a quick shine before going into the interview room.

BEFORE MOVING ON

1. I am a strong believer in creating and using checklists, no matter how familiar you are with the activity. Before your next interview, take a few minutes, a day or two before the meeting, to create a pre-interview checklist and review each item on the list. It's better to be over-prepared.

Chapter 20

Overcoming Interview Anxiety

"You have to rely on your preparation. You've got to … prepare more than anyone else, and put yourself in a position to succeed, and when the moment comes you got to enjoy, relax, breathe and rely on your preparation so that you can perform and not be anxious or filled with doubt."

- Steve Nash

MOST PEOPLE EXPERIENCE some performance anxiety before or during an interview. For some, it will be very minor like feeling a pit in your stomach, experiencing a dry mouth, or a pounding heartbeat. The good news is that the interviewers will not notice these symptoms.

Others may experience more acute symptoms like sweaty palms, trembling hands, and a shaking voice, things that can be detected.

Why do we experience anxiety?

For most people, interview anxiety is caused by the belief that the stakes are high. We believe that getting the job will help solve some (or many) of our problems. It means we can pay our bills, buy a new house, complete a move to a new city, or get out of a bad job situation.

We also know that the interview is very much a make-or-break situation, especially the first interview. We know that if we blow that interview by being nervous, we will not get a second chance. Our brain goes to:

If I screw up,
- I won't be able to pay my bills.
- I won't be able to move out of my crummy apartment.
- I won't be able to move to the city I've always wanted to live in.
- I will have to stay in my lousy job.

That thought-process creates a lot of stress and pressure, resulting in nervousness. If you don't believe me, just think of times when you interviewed for jobs that you were only moderately interested in. Since the stakes seemed lower, I bet you weren't as nervous.

How to stay calm

According to the Salisbury University (Maryland) Career Services, some of the most common symptoms of interview anxiety are:

Shaking legs	Nightmares
Wobbly knees	Eating too much
Racing thoughts	Eating too little
Irrational thoughts	Muscle tension
Feeling nausea	Pounding heart
Shortness of breath	Voice may crack
Sweaty palms	Difficulty concentrating
Headaches	Insomnia
Racing heartbeat	Dizziness
Voice constriction	Rushing
Poor motor control	Memory loss
Trembling hands	Cold palms
Stiff movements	Distorted sense of time
Numbness in body	Stumbling and bumbling
Dry throat	Blushing
Freezing up	Negative thinking

While you may not be able to fully overcome your interview anxiety, there are some techniques you can use to mask the symptoms.

Being prepared is the most effective way to cope with anxiety. Coming to the interview room with your research complete and ready to explain how your skills and qualifications line up with the job that you're applying for will make you feel confident. You should also learn about the people who are interviewing you by researching their bios. Believe me, you will impress an interviewer if you can mention something about their background.

The second way to stay calm is to eliminate the possibility of any last minute panic. Take care of everything the day before such as printing extra copies of your resume, figuring out your wardrobe and making sure that your clothes are clean and pressed. It's also wise to map out your route so you know where you're going and how long it will take you to get there.

Another useful way to deal with anxiety is to know that you are a good candidate. Remember that someone has read your cover letter and resume and checked you out online and decided they would like to meet you. Interviewers don't want to waste their time or anyone else's. Knowing that you are a candidate worth meeting should give you a boost of confidence going into an interview.

Practice makes perfect

One of the best ways to reduce your anxiety is to rehearse by conducting a mock interview. In the next chapter, we will speak about the value in anticipating the questions you will be asked. Ask a friend, family member, or mentor to play the role of the interviewer and pose questions to you. Critique your answers and ask your friend or family member to do the same. Like most things, the more we practice our interviewing skills the better we become. Also consider videotaping your mock interview to really *see* your strengths and weaknesses.

Think of the interview as a two-way street

Remember: it is possible you will decline the offer should it be made to you. From your point of view, the interview is also an opportunity to determine if the job is right for you, if the salary is in line with what you want, and if the work will be satisfying and challenging. Knowing that you are deciding whether the job is right for you, while the employer is deciding whether you are right for them, is the great equalizer.

Wear your favourite clothes

Let's face it, we all have clothes we feel better in. Maybe it's the shape, the style, or a colour that makes us look better. Choose clothes that make you feel good and comfortable. If you have to wear a tie, make sure that your shirt collar size is large enough that you don't strangle yourself when you button the top button of your shirt. Remember, this is no time to experiment with a new look.

Practise relaxation techniques

While I have not been on a job interview for many years, there are many days when I want to be at the top of my game. Perhaps I am making a presentation, meeting with a new client, or giving a media interview. Whatever the reason, I want to be feeling and looking my best. For me that means going for a run or a workout that morning. I know that if I have exercised and broken a sweat, my body and my mind will feel great. Exercise clearly helps me relax.

For you, it might be something else. It might be a brisk walk in a park, quiet time in private, or even meditation. Understand what makes you feel good and do things that make you feel good before an interview.

BEFORE MOVING ON

1. Think about past interviews when your level of anxiety might have caused you to under-perform in the interview. If you were doing those interviews over again, how could you have prepared differently?

Chapter 21

Anticipate the Questions
You'll Be Asked

"To be prepared is half the victory."

- Miguel de Cervantes

THE MOST EFFECTIVE way to prepare for an interview is to anticipate the questions you are going to be asked. If you do this well, you will rarely be thrown off guard during an interview.

But how do you figure that out?

Pretend you are the interviewer. Take the job description or job posting and review the requirements of the job. From that list, prepare a list of questions you would ask a candidate if the roles were reversed.

Candidates who do their homework should be able to predict almost every interview question or at least a version of most questions asked. To help you with that task, I have prepared a list of possible interview questions categorized by topic. Think carefully about how you might answer each one:

Opening
- Tell me about yourself.
- How did you hear about the position?
- What do you know about our organization?

Education
- Tell us about your educational background
- What prompted you to study (accounting)?
- What courses did you find the easiest? The hardest?
- What courses or seminars have you taken beyond formal schooling?
- Who were your favourite instructors and why?

Work history

- Tell us about your work history.
- What did you like the most (least) about your previous job?
- Describe the major accomplishments of your last job.
- Why did you leave your last job?
- Describe your successes on this job.
- Why was there a gap in your employment between *[date]* and *[date]*?
- What did you like most (least) about the people you worked with? Why?
- What has been your biggest professional disappointment?
- Have you ever been asked to leave a position?

Level of interest

- Why do you want to work for us?
- Why should we hire you?
- Why do you want to leave your current company?
- Why are you looking for a new job?
- Why do you believe you are qualified for this position?
- How long would you work for us if we hired you?

Personal interests

- What do you do outside of work?
- What hobbies do you have?
- How do you spend your spare time?
- What is your favorite website?
- What is the last book you read?
- What is the last movie you saw?
- What countries have you travelled to?
- What magazines and books do you read?
- What community activities are you involved with at present?

Knowledge of company

- Who are our major competitors?
- What are the three biggest issues facing our company?

Career plans

- Where do you see yourself in 5 years? 10 years?
- What are your career goals?
- Tell me about your dream job.
- What are you looking for in a job?
- What type of work culture suits you best?

Management style
- Describe your management style.
- How many people have you supervised?
- What would your employees say about you?
- What are your strengths?
- What are your weaknesses?

Values
- What are your personal values and how do they drive your day-to-day work?

Weaknesses
- What are your shortcomings?
- What are you doing to improve these shortcomings?
- When have these weaknesses been a problem for you?
- What are three things your former manager would like you to improve on?
- What was your biggest failure?
- If I called your boss right now and asked him what is an area that you could improve on, what would he say?

Learning from others
- Who are your role models and what have you learned from them?
- Which boss did you look up to most? Why?

Communication skills
- How would you describe your own communication skills?
- Describe a situation when you were able to strengthen a relationship by communicating effectively. What made your communication effective?

Mistakes
- Tell me about one of your failures.
- What have you learned from mistakes on the job?

Working hours
- Are you willing to travel?
- Would you work 40+ hours a week?

Self-motivation
- What motivates you?
- What gets you up in the morning?
- Are you ambitious?
- What motivates you to do your best on the job?

Everybody Has Their Own Style

Lots of managers have their own tried-and-true models for asking interview questions. In an interview with the New York Times (Sunday, April 14, 2014) Brad Smith, CEO of Intuit, the software company, says that he starts every interview with an icebreaker. He says to the candidate, "I want you and I to get to know each other. So in the next three minutes, I'd like you to take me from where you were born to where you are now, and share with me the major inflection points in your life that you think have helped you form who you are today."

Smith goes on to then ask, "Tell me about an area that your last boss and the one before that said, 'This is your biggest area for improvement.'" By asking this question, he is attempting to see if the candidate will open up to him and be honest about shortcomings.

From there, he asks "What is the single biggest business mistake you've made, and what was the lesson you took from that?" He says he asks this question to see if they are willing to learn.

Lastly, he tries to determine if there are any reasons why the candidate would not accept an offer if one was made. So, he'll ask "Why would you not join our company?" He says this question is designed to identify concerns the individuals might have so that he can deal with them.

Based on an interview by Adam Bryant, The New York Times, April 13, 2014.

Managing others
- Have you ever had to fire someone? How did you feel about that?
- Can you outline for us your approach in coaching and mentoring staff?

Relocation
- Would you be willing to relocate if required?

Qualifications for the job
- Don't you think you are overqualified for this position?
- Tell us how your skills match our requirements.
- How do you propose to compensate for your lack of experience?

- If you were hiring a person for this job, what qualities would you look for?
- Why do you think you would do well at this job?

Accomplishments
- When you look back, what are your most significant accomplishments?
- What would you look to accomplish in the first 30, 60, and 90 days?
- Describe a project you were particularly proud of accomplishing and why.

Work ethic
- How would others describe your work ethic?
- What is your philosophy towards work?

Salary
- What are your salary expectations?
- How much are you making now?

Closing
- What questions haven't I asked you?
- What questions do you have for me?
- If offered the job, when could you begin?
- Are you applying for other jobs right now?
- Tell us why this job appeals to you?
- How does this job fit with your long-term career plans?

Be Prepared For Behavioral Interview Questions

Most of the previous questions are "traditional" interview questions. Virtually everyone asks them and they definitely have a place in most interviews.

Behavioural interviewing, on the other hand, is based on the premise that past performance is the best predictor of future performance. The underlying assumption is that if you behaved a certain way in the past, there is a high probability that you will behave the same way again given similar circumstances.

The downside with asking traditional interview questions is that they allow candidates to answer hypothetically: to say what they *think* they would do when faced with a particular situation. For example, let's say an interviewer asks you the following question:

> What would you do if there was a disagreement between two employees you were supervising?

Ask Gerry

Q. I was let go in my last job and I feel very embarrassed about it. I have never been dismissed before and I have never been unemployed. I know the question will come up in interviews. How would you suggest I handle it?

A. Most certainly the stigma associated with being fired and unemployed is far less than it used to be. With all the corporate restructuring that has taken place, almost everybody has been downsized or right-sized (whatever you want to call it) at one time or another.

If the question arises, you must deal with it truthfully. Explain what happened even if it is uncomfortable. Long, carefully rehearsed answers never go over well. It makes it seem like you are hiding something. Your best strategy is to be direct and brief. And don't point blame at your former boss or employer. Keep the tone positive, emphasizing that the past is behind you and you are moving forward.

The answer to this question could be completely hypothetical. That's because you're describing something that has yet to happen. There is no real way for the employer to know how you would handle that situation if actually faced with it. It's not that you're lying. You're just describing the way that you think you'd react. But you don't really know until you encounter that situation. That's the problem with traditional interview questions.

By asking for an example of past behaviour, the interviewer can quickly determine what skills already exist.

For example, say the same question was framed as a behavioural question. It would go something like:

> Tell me about a time when there was a disagreement between two employees that you were supervising. What was the problem between the two employees? What actions did you take? What was the result?

You will note that the previous question actually has three parts:

P – What was the <u>problem</u> (or situation) you faced?
A – What <u>actions</u> (or steps) did you take to understand and resolve the problem?
R – What was the <u>result</u> (or outcome) of your actions?

A sample answer to this behavioural question might go something like this:

> I manage a department with seven employees. About six months ago, I noticed there was tension between two of my employees and it appeared they were not even speaking to each other unless absolutely necessary. Then other employees began telling me how awkward it was for them to have two of their co-workers not talking to each other. It is a small staff and it is important that we have a collegial work environment.
>
> So I met with both of them at the same time to explain that this behaviour was not acceptable and that I intended to meet with each one separately to gain their respective perspectives on the problem. In the separate meetings, I discovered the source of their disagreement was one employee's off-handed comments about the quality of the other person's work. The second employee was offended by her co-workers remarks and this led to the silence between both individuals.
>
> When I explained to the first employee that remarks like this were not appropriate, he acknowledged that he was out of line and should not have worded his comments the way he did. He offered to apologize, which he did, and explained that he really wanted a harmonious relationship with all his co-workers.
>
> The second employee thanked him and accepted his apology and said she too was committed to a cooperative, respectful workplace. They've been getting along like best friends since then.

You can tell from that answer this person appears to have decent supervisory qualities. You could also assume that if faced with a similar situation again, he would probably handle it the same way. That is why employers use behavioural interview questions in most interviews.

How to prepare for behavioural interviews

Assuming that you have access to the job ad or description, it is fairly easy to prepare for behavioural interviews. A careful review of the information provided will tell you what skills the employer is seeking. You can then reasonably assume they will design questions to find out if you have these skills. Once you have a good sense of the questions, you can easily prepare your answers.

Here is a list of several possible behavioural questions to aid your preparation. When thinking of answers, don't forget about PAR!

P – Problem
A – Action
R – Result

Adaptability
- Describe a major change that occurred in a job that you held. How did you adapt to this change?
- Tell us about a situation in which you had to adjust to changes over which you had no control. How did you handle it?

Ambiguity
- Have you ever worked in a situation where the rules and guidelines were not clear? Tell me about it. How did you feel about it? How did you react?

Ambition
- Describe a project or idea that was implemented primarily because of your efforts. What was your role? What was the outcome?

Analytical thinking
- Tell us about a time when you had to analyze mountains of data and make a recommendation. What kind of thought process did you go through? What was the reasoning behind your decision?

Attention to detail
- Do you prefer to work with the "big picture" or the "details" of a situation? Give me an example of an experience that illustrates your preference.
- Tell us about a situation where attention to detail was important in accomplishing an assigned task.

Building relationships
- It's important to build good relationships at work but sometimes it doesn't happen. Can you tell me about a time when you were not able to build a successful relationship with a difficult person?

Communication
- Describe a situation when you were able to strengthen a relationship by communicating effectively. What made your communication effective?

- Give me an example of a time when you were able to successfully communicate with another person, even when that individual may not have personally liked you or vice versa.
- Tell us about a time when you and your supervisor disagreed but you still found a way to get your point across.
- Tell us about an experience where you had to speak up in order to be sure that other people knew what you thought or felt.

Conflict resolution
- Describe a time when you took personal responsibility for a conflict and initiated contact with the individual(s) involved to resolve the situation.

Decision making
- Everyone has made some poor decisions or has done something that just did not turn out right. Has this happened to you? What happened?
- Give an example of when you had to make a decision with little information.
- Tell us about a time when you had to defend a decision you made even though other important people were opposed to your decision.

Delegation
- How do you make the decision to delegate work? And then tell us how you go about delegating work?

Diversity
- Give a specific example of how you have helped create an environment where differences are valued, encouraged and supported.
- Tell us when you successfully adapted to a culturally different environment.

Flexibility
- How have you adapted your style when it was not meeting the objectives of a situation?

Follow-up
- How do you keep track of what your subordinates are doing? What do you do if they are off track?

Initiative
- Give me an example of when you had to go above and beyond the call of duty in order to get a job done.

Interpersonal skills
- Tell us about the most difficult or frustrating individual that you've ever had to work with and how you managed to work with them.
- What have you done in past situations to contribute toward a teamwork environment?

Ask Gerry

Q. I was in a behavioral interview not long ago. I was pretty good at providing examples, but there were a couple of questions that really stumped me. The interviewer told me to take my time while I thought of an answer. Frankly, I found the silence quite uncomfortable. It seemed like an eternity before I could come up with anything. Is there anything you can recommend to help me deal with this awkward silence?

A. Work on being comfortable with silence. A good interviewer will not let you off the hook by withdrawing the question or leading you with examples. One strategy you might try is to ask if you can come back to the question later. The interviewer will probably say yes. Hopefully, if you have done your preparation in advance, you should not encounter this situation too often. But in the end, if you cannot think of anything, the interviewer will conclude that you lack the skill.

Innovation
- Describe a time when you came up with a creative solution to a problem in your past work.
- Sometimes you have to break from a routine, standardized way of doing things. Give an example of when you were able to successfully develop a new approach.

Integrity
- Tell us when your trustworthiness was challenged. How did you react?
- Tell us when you had to handle a tough problem that challenged your ethics.

Judgment
- Give an example of a time when you used good judgment to solve a problem.

Leadership
- Give me an example of a time when you motivated your co-workers or subordinates.

Listening
- Give me an example of a time when you made a mistake because you did not listen well to what someone had to say.

Motivation
- Have you ever had a subordinate whose work was always marginal? How did you deal with that person? What happened?

Negotiating
- Describe the most challenging negotiation in which you were involved. What did you do? What were the results for you and the other party?

Organizational
- What do you do when your schedule is suddenly interrupted? Give an example.

Performance management
- Give me an example of how you have been successful at empowering either a person or a group of people into accomplishing a task.
- When do you give positive feedback to people? Tell me about the last time you did so.

Personal effectiveness
- There are times when we are under extreme pressure on the job. Tell about a time when you were under serious pressure and how you handled it.

Persuasion
- Describe a situation where you were able to use persuasion to successfully convince someone to see things your way.

Planning
- How do you schedule your time? Set priorities? How do you handle doing twenty things at once?

Presentation
- Tell us about the most challenging presentation you have made. What was the topic? What made it difficult? How did you handle it?

Problem solving
- Describe the most difficult working relationship you've had with an individual. What specific actions did you take to improve the relationship? What was the outcome?
- Have you ever been caught unaware by a problem or obstacles that you had not foreseen? What happened?

Project management
- Tell us about a time when you influenced the outcome of a project by taking a leadership role.

Relationships
- What would your co-workers or staff say is the most frustrating thing about your relationship with them?

Self-awareness
- Can you recall a time when you were less than pleased with your performance?
- If there was one area you've always wanted to improve upon, what would that be? In what ways are you trying to improve yourself?
- What was the most useful criticism you ever received?

Selecting people
- What have you done to develop and improve the skills of your subordinates? Provide an example.
- What was your biggest mistake in hiring someone? What happened? How did you deal with the situation?

Strategic thinking
- Tell us about a time when you anticipated the future and made changes to current operations to meet those future needs.

Stress management
- What kind of events cause you stress on the job?
- What was the most stressful situation you have faced? How did you deal with it?

Teamwork
- Describe a team experience you found disappointing. What would you have done to prevent this?
- Give an example of how you worked effectively with people to accomplish an important result.

Time Management
- Describe a situation that required you to do a number of things at the same time. How did you handle it? What was the result?

BEFORE MOVING ON

1. Keep all of these questions handy and be sure to review them before your next interview. Obviously you will never be asked all of them nor is this an all-inclusive list of possible questions. There are many others that might be asked. However being ready to answer these questions will prepare you better than most candidates.

Chapter 22

Leave a Lasting Impression
to Stand Out

"It's not the impression you make, it's the impression you leave."

— Maryln Schwartz, *New Times in The Old South*

EMPLOYERS WANT TO hire people they like and whom they feel will be a good fit for their organization. In fact, employers often reject candidates who possess strong technical skills but come across as arrogant, in favour of candidates who are likeable but with fewer technical skills.

Leah Eichler writing in her *Women@Work column* in *The Globe & Mail* referenced research that has been conducted in this area by Tiziano Casciaro, associate professor of organizational behaviour at University of Toronto Rotman School of Management. Dr. Casciaro has found that employers consider both competency and likeability when hiring. However, she also suggests that "when faced with the choice of competent jerk and loveable fool, most [employers] choose the loveable fool."

Now I know most of you are both competent and likeable, but it never hurts to have a few pointers.

When you arrive

Your interview starts the moment you walk in the door – not the door of the interviewer's office but the front door of the building.

It goes without saying (but I am saying it anyway) that you must be on time for your interview. Your best strategy is to scout the location a few days before so that you know exactly where it is and how long it will take you to get there. Plan to arrive outside the building about thirty minutes before your actual interview time to give yourself the chance to unwind, straighten your tie, fix your hair, or whatever. You can go into the building about ten to fifteen minutes before your actual interview time.

Having said that, don't arrive more than 30 minutes before the interview. Doing so conveys that you have nothing better to do. It could also be interpreted as disrespectful of others' time particularly if you end up chatting with the front-desk receptionist for this time.

Bring the name and contact information of the person you're meeting along with you just in case you get delayed by car troubles or traffic. You can send them a quick note or call to say you're going to be a few minutes late. They will understand.

Once you're inside the door, you are being judged. Other employees might be nosing around, curious about the candidates. For sure, the receptionist is judging you on how friendly you are. So always be on your best behaviour.

Handshake

One of the best ways to make a sure-fire good first impression is with a strong handshake and friendly greeting. The rules of handshakes are well-known but not always followed (for some reason):

- Stand up to greet the person (it still amazes me at how many people remain seated as I extend my hand to them);
- Make sure your palm is dry and cool (not sweaty, in other words);
- Make eye contact and maintain it throughout the greeting;
- State an appropriate greeting, such as "Nice to meet you, _____";
- Smile comfortably;
- Give a firm, confident squeeze but don't break his hand;
- Hold the handshake for two to three seconds; and
- Don't give a two-handed handshake EVER, as it comes across as insincere.

If you pass the handshake test, you're halfway to getting the job. Well, maybe not quite halfway, but it's a good start!

Seating

When you enter the interviewer's office, she may gesture for you to sit in a pre-assigned seat, such as across from her desk or at the head of the table. Don't argue, just go there.

If, however, the interviewer offers you a choice of seating, always opt for the more upright chair if there is one. Big, soft, comfy chairs are great for watching TV, but they're risky in an interview setting. That's because they can be difficult to get out of and awkward, particularly if you're a woman wearing a dress or skirt.

Also look for an inconspicuous spot to place your belongings such as a briefcase or purse. Never place them on the table or interviewer's desk, or even your lap. Instead, just place them on the floor beside your chair.

Once seated, relax and lean slightly forward in a comfortable pose. This gives the message that you are confident, interested and ready to go on with the interview.

Dress

I was interviewing candidates once for an executive director position for an alcohol addiction recovery centre. This facility was located in an old house in the heart of a mid-sized city. It was not exactly a five-star hotel with concierge service, if you know what I mean.

In an example of how not to dress for an interview, one of the candidates arrived dressed in a dark blue business suit, white dress shirt with French cuffs and cufflinks, an expensive tie, and winged-tip black shoes. His attire screamed Wall Street (or Bay Street) investment banker more than anyone I'd seen, and illustrated how important it is to dress appropriately for the audience you're meeting.

That means you don't overdress or underdress for an interview. Guy Kawasaki in his book *Enchantment* said it well: "Dress for a tie (no pun intended), not a victory or a loss." Overdressing the way our friend did symbolizes superiority, trying to show he has money or power or great taste. True, this probably is not the message he was trying to convey. Yet it comes across as that way and immediately disconnects him from the interviewer. Similarly, underdressing such as wearing jeans and t-shirt and sandals in a corporate setting, gives off a message of disrespect like, "I am going to dress anyway I want, I don't care what you think."

Neither work. Which is why Kawasaki says dress for a "tie." Simply match your dress to your audience as closely as you can when heading to an interview. And, by the way, it's okay to ask the person who calls you to book the interview time, "How should I dress for the interview?" If nothing else, it shows you care.

Voice

When we're nervous, we tend to speak faster than we normally do. So be conscious of your speed of speech during interviews and deliver what you have to say in a controlled and deliberate manner. The pace and tone may seem draggy to you but it will come across perfectly.

Also, avoid laughing at your own witty comments. You run the risk that no one else finds them funny and you'll look like a fool. Better still, forget the witty comments altogether. Just because you find them funny doesn't mean anyone else will.

One way to control your voice tone and pitch (particularly at the beginning of an interview) is to breathe and pause before answering a question. Not only does this give you more time to reflect on your answer, it also helps you relax so your tone and pitch is the real you.

And, if offered something to drink, like coffee, tea, juice or water, always accept water, even if you're not thirsty. When we're tense, our mouths tend to dry out so a good glass of water will keep the pipes lubricated. Avoid coffee, tea and juice because the consequences of spilling your drink are more severe than if you spilled water.

Eye contact

There are two rules of thumb to remember about eye contact during job interviews.

First, when the interviewer is speaking to you, maintain 100% eye contact with him to show you are actively listening. While doing so, nodding your head (as if in agreement with what he is saying) or saying, "uh huh" or "yes" periodically, will further impress him that you are listening and understand what he is saying. Looking down or away suggests a lack of interest in what he is saying and makes him feel disconnected from you. Even if you have notes in front of you that you want to refer to, avoid looking down as it will leave the impression that you are not listening.

Second, when you are the one speaking, you should maintain eye contact with the interviewer for about 75% of the time and for not longer than 10 – 15 seconds at a time before looking away. The reason it is okay to look away once in a while when speaking is that it gives the impression that you are collecting your thoughts in order to continue the conversation.

You should avoid over–using eye contact, such as maintaining 100% direct contact, as it can come across as lecturing. Likewise, less eye contact or frequent loss of eye contact during an answer will leave the impression that you are not telling the truth.

If you are taking notes or referring to information in front of you, it is fine to look down to check them. However, do this only when neither of you is speaking, such as between questions.

A quick note about panel interviews: When answering a question, start your answer by looking at the person who asked the question, glance periodically at the other panelists during your answer, and finish up your answer looking back at the original questioner.

Hands and legs

Your hands and legs can become a major distraction during an interview and the funny thing is – you might not even know it!

I once sat in an interview where the candidate spent almost the entire interview clearing away little specks of dust on the interview table. Needless to say, we had a pretty clean table by the end of the interview and the candidate proceeded no further in the process.

If you're not sure what to do with your hands, just rest them loosely on your lap or in the table. Most of us tend to gesture with our hands when we speak and you should feel comfortable doing this to emphasize your points, although these gestures should be controlled.

Some people get very emphatic when speaking. If you have this tendency, resist the temptation to gesture wildly. You will come across as too emotional. Likewise, try to avoid folding your arms across your chest, which could be perceived as defensive or close-minded, and touching your face or your hair, which could be interpreted as nervousness or anxiety.

As far as your legs are concerned, keep them firmly on the ground or crossed at the knee. Like hands and arms, too much leg movement can be distracting and suggest nervousness.

Ask Gerry

Q. I applied for this job and the employer asked for references before I was even interviewed. I find this practice very unusual, not to mention inconvenient for my references especially since I didn't even know if I was interested in the job or if they were interested in me. What would you suggest I do?

A. It is unusual – but not unheard of – for an employer to ask for references prior to the first interview. I would caution against providing references especially if you are currently employed and your employer is not aware you are looking for another job. Not only is this inconvenient for your references, as you state, but it could be very embarrassing to you if word got back to your employer. If you still feel you must send them along in advance, you might consider telling that prospective employer, by phone or in writing, to refrain from contacting these references without your prior knowledge.

The interviewer's body language

As if worrying about your own body language isn't enough, you also have to pay attention to what the interviewer is communicating non-verbally.

For example, loss of eye contact or fiddling with hands might indicate that you have already answered their question sufficiently and they want you to wrap up your answer. A furrowed brow might indicate they are not understanding your answer and you might want to simplify what you are saying. A frown might be an indicator they disapprove of what they are hearing and you should switch subjects.

Mimicking

One technique that sales people use to forge relationships with customers is to mimic their customer's movements. What this means is that if the customer leans forward, the sales person leans forward. If the customer rests his head on his hand, the sales person does the same.

I believe this is a technique that, if executed successfully, can be an effective way for a candidate to strengthen a bond with the interviewer. The key is to be subtle. Observe what the interviewer is doing: Is he speaking quickly? Is he sitting back? Has he crossed his legs? Then without being too obvious, mimic these actions.

Or, if the interviewer makes an important point, repeat that same point a few minutes later. It demonstrates to the interviewer that you are listening.

BEFORE MOVING ON

1. One way to learn how to use non-verbal language (i.e. body language) effectively is by observing others. Sit back and watch how others behave non-verbally – perhaps at a coffee shop or in a business meeting at work – and think about what they are saying through their actions.

Chapter 23

Avoid Jargon

"The finest language is ... made up of simple unimposing words."

- George Eliot

WHEN INTERFACING WITH the interviewer, your optimal strategy out of the gate is to utilize words that leverage your best assets and focus on your core competencies. The words you speak must convey a bold, nimble, flexible approach to doing business in the employer's space. If you need to, circle back and show them how you can re-purpose yourself to meet their corporate metrics. At the end of the day, the interviewer should not have to drill down to figure out if you can hit the ground running. Plain, simple language is the optimal way to foster a relationship with the interviewer and gain traction over your competitors.

What? Didn't understand that paragraph?

No worries, here is what it really means:

In an interview, nothing turns off an interviewer more than a candidate using corporate jargon that no one understands. It can also be offensive to the interviewer who may think you are trying to show you are smarter than them. Stick to plain, simple language. Explain your strengths and skills. Tell them exactly how you will help them achieve their goals. You can't go wrong. The interviewer should not have to work hard to figure out what you mean. You will have an advantage over other candidates.

Unfortunately, irritating buzzwords and phrases are used all the time in business. Here is my list of the most annoying jargon terms that under no circumstances should find their way into your cover letter, resume, or interview. Special thanks to my Twitter followers and LinkedIn connections for their fine contributions.

Actionable	Guesstimate	Optimize
Air tight	Hit the ground running	Paradigm shift
At the end of the day	Human capital	Re-purpose
Bandwidth	Impacting	Right-size
Bring our A game	Incentivize	Sacred cow
Circle back	Interfacing	Scalable
Core competency	Leading edge	Silos
Customer-facing	Let's do lunch	Synergize
Drill down	Level playing field	Strategic anything
Face time	Leverage	Subject matter expert
Foster	Mission-critical	Take it off line
Functionality	Monetize	Outside the box
Gain traction	Operationalize	Traction
Go forward basis	Optics	Value add

BEFORE MOVING ON

1. Eliminate these words from your vocabulary. Simple. Promise never to use them anywhere!

Chapter 24

How to Respond to Illegal Interview Questions

**"I usually make up my mind about a man in ten seconds,
and I very rarely change it."**

- Margaret Thatcher

ALL PROVINCES IN Canada as well as the federal government have laws that protect individuals from discriminatory hiring practices.

This means that, when hiring, employers cannot discriminate in any way based on age, race, colour, religion, creed, sex, sexual orientation, physical or mental disability, ethic, national or aboriginal origin, family or marital status, irrational fear of contracting an illness, source of income, association with protected groups or individuals, and political belief, affiliation or activity. Further, employers cannot ask any questions about any of these topics unless it is specifically relevant to your ability to do the job.

Quite often employers get mixed up and ask illegal questions unintentionally. For example, let's say an employer wants to ensure all applicants, because of the nature of the job, are able to work overtime, on short notice, and travel frequently overnight. Most people think that having children, particularly young children, could impair a person from working these extra hours. An employer, not thinking about how the question is posed might then ask: "How many children do you have?" That's an illegal question.

However if it is re-phrased to: "This job requires overtime on short notice and frequent overnight travel. Is that okay with you?" Then the question is fine because that's a job requirement.

Examples of questions about family and marital status that an employer, by anyone's definition, cannot ask legally include:

Are you planning on having any more children?
Are you pregnant now?
How does your spouse feel about you taking this job?
That's a pretty ring. Did your husband give it to you?
What child care arrangements have you made for your children?

Questions about age is another touchy area. Some employers, particularly when hiring for senior management positions, want to think a person will stay in the job for ten years or more. If they believe that most people plan to retire in their mid-sixties, they might be reluctant to hire someone older than 55 (or even younger.) This sometimes causes them to ask illegal questions like: "How old are you?", "What year where you born?", "When did you go to high school?" The only time when age is relevant to the job is when the job requires someone to be a certain minimum legal age, such as bartender position. In that instance, it is okay to ask for proof of age as it is a requirement of the job.

Say you walk with a limp or with the aid of a cane due to a physical disability. The employer is not able to ask about your disability. He is however permitted to say, as he should with every candidate: "This job requires that you be able to lift 50 pound packages and place them on shelves in the warehouse. Are you able to do this?"

With all these questions, whether it is about age, ability, family, race or religion, the key question for you as a candidate is how should you respond if asked?

One effective way to deal with this is to ask yourself: Was this just an unintended gaffe by someone who didn't know any better? Or was it the result of real bias on the part of the person asking the question?

I know a woman, named Robyn, who in the course of being interviewed for a job had tea with the mostly-retired founder of a business, a gentleman in his early eighties. During their tea, he asked Robyn about her family and what ages her children were. While technically the questions were illegal, Robyn took no offense realizing that the founder was just being friendly and conversational and she chose to tell him her children were 8, 10 and 14. And she got the job.

However, if it feels to you that the question is purposely designed to bias the selection process, then you should ask yourself whether you really want to work for an employer who behaves this way. Are these the types of bosses that you would be proud to tell your friends about?

Alternatively you could politely ask, "Respectfully, how does that question relate to my ability to do the job?" Or, "How is that relevant to this job?"

The choice of whether or not to answer the question is yours.

My experience is that most employers are not out to discriminate against job applicants and that the questions they ask that fall into the "illegal" category are unintended. By simply pointing out that the question is illegal, most interviewers will realize immediately what they have done and withdraw the question.

I know of another woman who upon entering the interview room started out by saying to the employer, "I am 35 years old. I have two children who are looked after by a neighbour. My husband and I don't plan on having any more kids and he is fine if I have to travel with this job. Now let's just get on with this interview."

BEFORE MOVING ON

1. Give some thought as to how you might respond in the off chance you are asked one of these questions in an interview. As I said earlier, the question might be a deliberate, knowing attempt to ask an illegal question or it might be accidental – just part of normal conversation. Your response might differ in either scenario.

Chapter 25

Strange and Silly
Interview Questions

"If there are no stupid questions, then what kind of questions do stupid people ask? Do they get smart just in time to ask questions?"

- Scott Adams

AS IF INTERVIEWS weren't stressful enough already, once in a while interviewers will lob a bizarre question your way to see how you respond to an unexpected query. How you handle those questions says a lot about you, even though they fall into the "strange and silly" category.

Let's start with the stupidest questions (in my opinion), the ones supposedly designed to measure some aspect of your personality. Take, for example, this question: "If you were an animal, what animal would you be?"

Apparently if you answer tiger, lion, cougar, or some other type of strong animal, you have the needed aggressive tendencies to propel you to the corner office in no time flat. On the other hand, if you say lamb, cat, bunny rabbit, or anything cuddly or furry, you are destined for more passive jobs, such as an accountant or administrator. Heaven help you if you say you'd like to be a type of reptile.

As you have no doubt detected from my sarcasm, I do not think highly of these questions.

Here's one of the best answers that I've read to the question: "If you were a tree in the forest, what type of tree would you be?" The candidate answered, "I would be an ash tree. Because then I could make it into a baseball bat and whack you over the head for asking me such a stupid question."

Then, he walked out.

While I find that answer amusing, I wouldn't recommend taking that approach.

There are also sensible questions that are designed to test your thought process. In other words, they are designed to find out how you might go about arriving at the answer if you were given more time. Sometimes the interviewer asking the question doesn't even know the correct answer and actually doesn't care what it is. She is really only concerned with testing qualities like analytical and problem-solving abilities.

These questions are sometimes referred to as "Fermi questions," named after Enrico Fermi (1901 – 1954), the renowned Italian physicist who, along with Robert Oppenheimer, created the atomic bomb.

In much of his work, Fermi relied on estimation by making justified guesses about problems that seemed impossible to answer given the limited amount of information available at the time. For example, Fermi is reported to have estimated the approximate strength of an atomic bomb detonated in testing based on the distance travelled by small pieces of paper dropped from his hand during the blast.

One of the interview questions that is cited as an example of a Fermi question is: "How many gas stations are there in North America?" Very few people (if any) would know the answer to that question off the top of their head. If you are asked one of these questions, the rule of thumb to follow is to pause and think carefully about what the interviewer is looking for. Then, proceed to answer.

For example, the gas stations question is clearly testing your problem-solving skills. So your answer might be something like this:

> I am not sure how many gas stations there are in North America. But's here is an approach I would take to figure it out. There are about 350 million people in the U.S. and about 35 million in Canada. That's 385 million people altogether. I would attempt to find out how many gas stations there are, say, for every 10,000 people. Let's assume there are four stations for every 10,000 people. That would mean there are about 150,000 stations in North America.

My note: You might need a calculator to figure that out if you are not so good at math but here's how you would do it:

- 385,000,000 / 10,000 = 38,500
- 38,500 x 4 = 154,000 stations

Always try to figure out a way to answer the question. Saying "I have absolutely no idea how many gas stations there are in North America" is not a good answer. Particularly if the interviewer gives you more rope by asking, "Well, then, how would you go about solving that problem if I gave you more time?" If you stupidly answer, "I don't know" to that question you might as well kiss your chances good-bye for that job.

Other questions designed to test your interests and character include:

- What is the most interesting place in the world you have visited and why?
- Tell me the last two books you have read and why you selected these ones?
- If you invited me over to your house for dinner, what would you make me?
- If you could trade places with any living person, who would that be and why?
- If you won $10 million in the lottery, what would you do with the money and how would your life change?
- Tell us what you do outside of work. How do you spend your spare time?

All of these questions are designed to learn more about the breadth and depth of your interests. Where you have visited might say something about your openness to other cultures and ideas. The types of books you read might indicate your knowledge of the employer's industry. What you would do with your lottery winnings might say something about your sense of social responsibility.

In all cases, be careful about how you answer these questions. You should consider adding some insight on why you answered the question a certain way. For example, "I spend all day long reading boring, complex legal documents so I unwind by reading trashy romance novels."

Still others are designed to determine how you see yourself:

- If there was a story written about you on the front page of the paper, what would the heading be?
- If you were to die tonight, what would your best friend say about you? What would your worst enemy say?
- If you were to assemble your last three bosses in a room to have a conversation about you, what would they say?
- On a scale of one to ten, how smart are you?
- In three words, how would you describe yourself?

Regardless of how you feel about some of these seemingly strange and silly questions, one thing they do is add a sense of spontaneity to the interview process. For far too long interviews have been based on a set of standardized questions.

BEFORE MOVING ON

1. It is difficult to prepare fully for these types of questions. The best strategy, when asked a "strange and silly" question, is to take a moment and try to figure out why the interviewer is asking the question. What quality is she trying to get at? Just like the "gas station" question was trying to get at your problem-solving and analytical skills, there is probably an underlying reason for the question. Figure this out before you start to answer.

Chapter 26

Being Interviewed by Skype

**"When I wrote 'The World Is Flat,' ... Facebook didn't exist;
Twitter was a sound; the cloud was in the sky; 4G was a parking place;
LinkedIn was a prison; applications were what you sent to college; and
Skype, for most people, was a typo."**

- Thomas Friedman, *New York Times*

*(Author's note: While my comments in this chapter mention Skype specifically,
the practices are applicable to any form of video conferencing.)*

IN MY SEARCH practice, I conduct a large number of first interviews by Skype. While I don't keep track of the exact numbers, my guess is that about 25 per cent of my interviews are conducted that way. I can only see this trend continuing as the travel costs to bring candidates in for initial meetings cannot be justified.

You should get ready for a Skype interview the same way as you would if you were being interviewed in person:

- Anticipate the questions you are going to be asked;
- Learn as much as you can about the company and the people who will be interviewing you;
- Develop several insightful questions you can ask during the interview; and
- Make some notes to make sure you address all your most important points.

In all likelihood, the employer is interviewing candidates who live near them, which places you and the other people on Skype at a slight disadvantage. However, here are some tips to help you rise to occasion.

Dress the part

The tendency in Skype interviews is to dress more casually than you would if you were in the employer's office. Big mistake! Even if you may prefer jeans and a t-shirt when working from home (who wouldn't?) you should always dress like the employer. Also, don't run the risk of wearing a shirt and tie (above the waist) and sweat pants (below the waist) thinking that your bottom half will not be seen. I once asked an interviewer to move his computer around so I could see him in a better light. When he got up to move, I could see he had his pyjama pants on. I wasn't too impressed.

Organize your surroundings

Maybe I am just nosy but I like to look at what's on the wall or bookcase behind the person and I often ask them about it. If they're in an interesting room, I sometimes ask them about that. Once I interviewed a person from Panama City, who had an apartment on the 20th floor overlooking the city and the water. I asked her to show it to me and it was spectacular.

On the other hand, I've interviewed people whose computer was in their bedroom and there was an unmade bed behind them and quite visible. Another fellow thought far enough ahead to put the dog outside before the interview. But what he didn't anticipate was the dog barking at the door throughout the entire interview. I finally had to tell him to take a moment and go take care of the dog because it was a clear distraction for him and us.

The bottom line here is: Be conscious of what your surroundings say about you and organize them accordingly.

Set up your computer so you look your best

A number of people use laptops on their desks and sit close to them. This means the person on the other end is looking up at you with a better view of your ceiling than of you. To overcome this problem, always make sure your computer is at eye level.

I use a laptop in my office. But for every Skype interview, I place one of those blue plastic recycling bins on my desk (upside down) and put my laptop on top of it. Now the camera of my laptop is at eye level. (No one says it makes me look any better, but I think it does.)

Don't forget that having correct lighting on you will make you look good. Just think back to when you've had portraits or other photos taken and how much care the photographer took to get the right lighting. While you won't have the luxury of a professional on standby, remember that overhead lighting or light from behind you will tend to wash out your face or even darken your face. The best type of lighting is natural light on your face. If you don't have natural light, use a small lamp, like a table lamp, to illuminate your face.

There are a number of other snippets to think about:

- Make sure you have strong Internet connection so there are no breaks or delays during the interview.

- Always get the interviewer's telephone number so that you can call them immediately if something happens to your connection.

- First impressions count so make sure your Skype user name and profile picture reflect you in a professional way. Please no pictures of your pets or images. If you want, you can always create a second Skype account for friends and family.

- Send your Skype contact details at least a day before the interview so the employer has plenty of time to accept.

- Don't be checking your email or browse online during the interview. The interviewer can see you and it's very obvious what you are doing. Actually, the best practice is to close out all other programs on your computer so you won't be tempted at all.

- Look at the camera, not yourself. We are all curious about how we look so there's a great temptation to look at yourself in the lower right hand corner. But doing so causes you to lose eye contact with the interviewer – not a good idea.

- Lastly, practice, practice, practice. I know you wouldn't consider giving a speech without rehearsing. The same rationale applies to being interviewed by Skype. Make sure you know how it works by practising with a friend online. Talking into a computer screen will feel awkward but a few rehearsals should ease those concerns. You will learn how to use the technology and how to present yourself professionally.

BEFORE MOVING ON

1. If you are not already a Skype user, in the next few days, commit to setting up your Skype account and testing it with a friend or family member so you know how it works. I can think of several times when I had a planned interview set up with a candidate (by Skype) but he or she had not bothered to figure it out beforehand. The result was they missed their interview and did not leave a favourable impression on me at all.

Chapter 27

Understanding the Hiring Manager's Objections

"Nothing will ever be attempted if all possible objections must first be overcome."

- Samuel Johnson

HIRING OBJECTIONS TEND to fall into the categories of:

- Pay *(We can't pay you what you want)*
- Experience *(You don't have enough experience)*
- Fit *(I am not sure you will fit with our team)*

In many respects an interview is like a sales call. You (the "salesperson") are trying to determine if the interviewer (the "customer") needs your services. In turn, the employer is trying to determine if you (the "salesperson"), can meet their needs and solve their problems.

There are many aspects to a successful sales call. But one of the key things is to anticipate possible buying objections and work to overcome them. Theoretically, in sales, if you overcome all the buyer's objections, they will have no choice but to purchase your product or service.

The same rationale applies to hiring. If you overcome any objections related to pay, experience and fit, you should move to the next stage of the hiring process.

Let's examine common objections and look at ways in which you might overcome them.

Objection #1: The job doesn't pay as much as you are looking for.

This is a totally understandable objection. Employers need to be aware of costs even if you are very well qualified for the job. It isn't an objection to your experience or skills. It is simply saying that they may not be able to afford you.

Be careful how you respond to this objection. You do not want to be drawn into an early salary negotiation. Instead you should try to deflect it so you can continue in the hiring process and hopefully establish that you are worth more than the original salary range.

You might try saying something like this:

> I am really interested in this job and the opportunity it offers for growth. I do recognize that salary is only one part of the total compensation package and I am willing to look at other areas of compensation, like benefits, vacation, performance bonuses, and professional development that may offset a lower salary than I had hoped for.

Although I wouldn't offer the following suggestion at the outset, you might also consider saying to the employer:

> I understand the job pays $70,000 and I was hoping for $80,000. I would be willing to start at $70,000 if you would agree to a six-month salary review and agree that that if my performance is fully satisfactory, you would then increase my pay to $80,000."

I have seen many salary deals come together using this approach. It indicates understanding and flexibility on your part and it minimizes the financial risk for the employer.

Objection #2: You don't have enough experience.

Sometimes employers mistakenly equate years of experience with the ability to do the job. Think of how many times you have seen job postings that say, "Must have at least five years of supervisory experience."

If you have four (or even three) years of good supervisory experience, you should not hesitate to apply. In fact, I recommend to employers to never stipulate in a posting the minimum number of years of experience candidates should have. The problem is if they do, very well-qualified candidates who have, say, four and a half years of experience, may decide not to apply assuming they have no chance at the job.

In any event, what should you do if an interviewer objects by saying you don't have enough experience to do the job?

I would suggest that you respond by stating your measureable accomplishments and responsibilities. For example:

> When I took over as supervisor, the client service team had ten employees and morale was at an all-time low. In the three years since I have been in that position, we've tripled our workforce to thirty employees and we've had no turnover in the past year. I am especially proud that the most recent employee satisfaction survey gave us a nine out of ten rating overall.

You might also suggest that the employer contact your references to attest to your skills as a supervisor. Or you might bring written letters of reference that you can present to the interviewer.

A word of caution: If you do not have the skills to do the job, do not minimize the importance of them by saying something like: "I am a quick learner and I am sure I will be able to pick up those skills quickly." While that statement may be true, it tends to highlight your shortcomings more.

Objection #3: I am not sure you will fit with the team.

This objection could be raised if the interviewer, based on her first impression of you, feels that you will not mesh with her current team members. Let's say for example that her current teams consists mostly of people with Type A personalities and her impression of you is that you are too laid back. She is concerned that you might not have what it takes to be successful in the role.

If an interviewer raises this objection, you should first clarify what she means by asking: "How would you describe the culture of your current team and what is your initial impression of me?"

Once you learn the basis of her concern, you are in a much better position to handle her objection by stating – with specific examples – how you have integrated well with other high-performing teams.

What to do if you cannot mitigate the objection?

Keep in mind that the mere fact that you've been called in for an interview means that employer feels (from your cover letter and resume) that you are close enough to what they are looking for to warrant an interview. So in most instances you will be able to mitigate their concerns.

However, if something has been overlooked and it becomes clear that their objection is valid, don't make stuff up. Don't lie or embellish your experience. It's far better to acknowledge that you lack a particular quality than to fabricate a story. It will always come back to haunt you.

Ask Gerry

Q. I was in an interview and could tell by the body language of the interviewer that he had concerns, although he didn't express any objections. I wasn't sure if I should ask him as I didn't want to run the risk of raising concerns if none existed. So I did nothing. Was this right?

A. It's not uncommon for interviewers to refrain from verbalizing concerns they might have about a candidate's experience or fit. Instead they often prefer to keep these objections hidden until they have had a chance to meet with all candidates. However be on the lookout for unstated objections expressed through frowns on their faces, folding their arms, sitting back, and many other ways in which people express their feelings through body language. If you observe these concerns, it would not be wise to probe further. (You could be wrong, after all.) Instead, sell yourself more by identifying all those measureable accomplishments that make you a good candidate for the job.

Chapter 28

Pass The Lunch Test

"When people you greatly admire appear to be thinking deep thoughts, they probably are thinking about lunch."

- Douglas Adams

WHICH FORK SHOULD I use? Is that my bread on the left? Or is it the piece on the right? Is it okay to have a beer? These may be simple questions to answer if you're having lunch with your friends, but if it's over lunch with a prospective employer, you better get it right.

Why is meal time etiquette so important?

The main reason employers take prospective candidates out to lunch or dinner is to evaluate their social skills and see how they will perform in real-life situations. Presumably this will only occur if you are being considered for a job that involves entertaining clients or some other outside group over a meal.

So, for example, if you're applying for a sales or business development role, where business is commonly conducted over lunch, there is a good chance this test will be part of your interview process. A serious etiquette miscue, such as having too much to drink, could possibly harm a deal with a client, so any prudent employer will want to test you in this area before making the decision to hire you.

Having lunch with a prospective employee also gives the employer the opportunity to evaluate your interpersonal skills. You are likely familiar with how to conduct business in a boardroom or an office where both parties tend to get down to business right away with little small talk beforehand. But over a meal it's different. Small talk is important and is more like a conversation than a question and answer format. So unless everyone is pressed for time, the work portion of the meal is left until dessert and coffee although you should follow the interviewer's lead and listen closely for when they wish to switch from casual conversation to more targeted questions about the job.

What should you know about etiquette?

1. When ordering, take the lead from your host. Ask them what they would recommend and then select something from that list. It gives you a sense of what price point they have in mind too. If they order, soup and salad for example, it would be inappropriate for you to order an appetizer and an expensive steak. Alternatively, if you know the restaurant you're going to, check out the menu online first so you know in advance what you're going to order. That way there will be no question about what to eat.

2. Always consider how easy a food will be to eat before ordering. You do not want the food to be a distraction and worse yet, you don't want to run the risk of it spilling on your suit. Always choose something that is light and easy to eat with a fork and knife, like fish and grilled vegetables or tossed salad. Avoid the more arduous foods (like spaghetti), foods you must eat with your fingers (like a big, messy sandwich), and food that may get stuck in your teeth (like spinach).

3. Do not order alcohol even if your host orders some. While you might feel this is being impolite to your host, if they order a drink and you do not, you should never feel obligated or pressured to consume alcohol. Besides, it's just smart to avoid it altogether in an interview setting.

4. Always be super-polite to the wait staff. An observant employer will be watching to see how you interact with your server. Unfortunately some people choose to disrespect servers, a bad move. Always listen to them, ask their advice on menu items, and say "please" and "thank you" as much as you can.

5. Mind your manners. Table manners do matter to many people and having good table manners might give you an advantage over other candidates. There are a host of things to remember. Some are obvious, or at least they should be, like 'don't speak with your mouth full', 'don't point with your fork' and 'wait until everyone has been served before starting to eat your meal.'

6. Remember BMW to simplify the place setting. (That's right, like the car). The place setting can be confusing but there are easy ways to keep track of things. Like BMW:

B – Bread is on your left;

M – Meal is in the middle;

W – Water (or wine) is on your right

Remembering which utensil to use can also be made easy. You simply start on the outside and work your way in. Your salad fork (the smaller one) will be on your far left, your entrée (main course) fork will be next to it. Your dessert spoon will be above your place setting and your knife on the right. When you are finished your meal, place your fork and knife together at an angle on your plate at the 10:00 and 4:00 positions. That signals to your server that you are finished and he can now take your plate away.

7. When everyone is seated, it's time to remove your napkin from the place setting, unfold it and place it on your lap. In some restaurants, the wait staff will do this for you. Your napkin should stay on your lap until the end of your meal. If you have to excuse yourself during the meal, simply fold your napkin and place it beside your plate until you return. Do the same at the end of the meal. Remember: your napkin is not to be used to clean your cutlery and I guarantee you will not get the job if you blow your nose in your napkin.

8. Eat soup by spooning it away from you. And as you tilt the bowl to get at those last drops, tip it away from you not toward you. Also remember to break your dinner roll into small pieces and eat it one piece at a time. Do not cut your dinner roll in half and butter both sides like so many people do.

Who pays?

The employer is always the one who picks up the tab. They invited you to lunch so they pay. Don't think that if you pay that it will improve your chances of being hired.

As the bill is being paid and lunch is wrapping up, make sure you discuss next steps which will help guide you on what to do next. And don't forget to thank your host for their time and their interest. And for the lunch!

Chapter 29

Questions You Can Ask
The Interviewer

**"The wise man doesn't give the right answers,
he poses the right questions."**

- Claude Levi-Strauss

YOU SHOULD ALWAYS remember that interviewing is a two-way street. The employer is asking questions of you to learn about your background, experience and skills to determine if you are a good fit for their organization. So it only stands to reason that you should ask questions about the job itself, the people you'll be working with, and the organization to figure out if they and the job are the right fit for you. In planning your questions, there are three important points to keep in mind.

Point #1:

Employers place a lot of value on the types of questions you ask them. Make sure they are strategic and insightful so that your questions leave a positive, lasting impression. Many employers have told me that the calibre of questions candidates ask of them are as important in the selection decision as the candidates' answers to their questions.

Point #2:

If you don't ask decent questions, you will leave the impression that you haven't prepared for the interview or are not interested in the job. I can't tell you how many times I've had candidates say to me, "Nope. I don't have any questions. I think you've answered everything for me." Impossible! Don't say that – always have questions ready to go. Even if you get the job, you might regret later on that you weren't inquisitive enough about what you might be facing.

Point #3:

Questions that focus on you are automatic deal-breakers. Especially in first interviews, never ask questions like:

What is the salary?
When can I expect to be promoted?
How many weeks' vacation do I get?

Eventually, you will get answers to these questions, so be patient. At all costs, avoid questions that suggest you are more concerned about what's in it for you than what you can contribute to the company.

Types of Questions You Can Ask

One easy way to think about the types of questions you can ask is to organize under the categories of *Job, People* and *Organization*. Here are ten examples of question under these categories:

The Job

What are the key responsibilities of the position?

This is an opportunity to learn more details about the job so you can make an informed decision about whether the job matches your skills and interests.

What are the biggest challenges of the job? (Or, what do you see as the priorities for the position?)

This question will help you uncover their problem areas and figure out how you can help them. For example, if they say the biggest challenge is their unmotivated workforce, you can tell them how you improved employee morale in your last job.

How would you describe the ideal candidate for the job?

This question will help you discover additional qualities they are looking for that might not have been listed in the job posting. Listen carefully, as people tend to name the most important qualities first.

How do you measure success (or performance) in this job?

This question will help you identify their performance metrics. Knowing what is important to them will help you explain how you achieved or exceeded your performance targets in the past.

Ask Gerry

Q. I was interviewed for a job last week. They must have liked me because they have just invited me in for a second interview and asked me to make a presentation at this interview. How should I prepare for this?

A. Congratulations! You've made it past the first round. That means you've met all or most of the technical requirements of the job. Now the employer is attempting to measure your other qualities to determine if you are the right candidate for their organization. By asking you to do a presentation, they are probably trying to measure your skills in communication, public speaking, stress management, charisma and persuasion.

One of the big mistakes people make in these situations is focusing too much on preparing a PowerPoint (or similar) set of slides. In fact, "making a presentation" doesn't always mean "preparing a PowerPoint." You might be just as effective speaking to the group without use of visual aids. You can make that decision based on the situation. But, mostly, figure out what the employer is trying to achieve when asking you to make a presentation and design your presentation around that answer.

The People

What are the expectations of the supervisor?

This question will help you clarify what the immediate boss expects from the new hire. They might explain their answer by telling you about their expectations for the first 30 days, 60 days, 90 days, and year. If they don't, ask them that question specifically.

How engaged are the employees in the department?

This question will help you gain insight into overall morale and help you decide if you want to join their company, should you be offered the job.

What do you like most about working here?

This is an interesting way to get the interviewer to share her personal perspective on why it is a good place to work.

The Organization

Where do you see the company being in five years?

This type of detail is rarely included in the job posting so ask the interviewer about her longer-term plans. This will help you decide whether you fit.

How would you describe the culture in the organization?

This question will give you a better sense of the work style and overall atmosphere in the office. But take this with a grain of salt. Many employers say that they encourage teamwork, yet they work behind closed doors.

What are the biggest issues facing the company right now?

This question is a well-placed, strategic level question. You can be assured these issues are what the CEO is focused on right now.

Final Tips to Remember

Be conscious of the interviewer's time and be sure to ask how much time they have available for your questions. While it's great to bring a long list of questions to the interview, it's quite likely that you only have time to ask three or four.

To wrap up the meeting, it's okay to ask about the next steps in the interview process. This question shows you are enthusiastic about moving forward in the process and it is a wonderful way to conclude your interview.

BEFORE MOVING ON

1. Think about the types of questions you asked in your last interview. Were they insightful and strategic? Do you think they added to the impression you left with the interviewers? Before your next interview, structure questions along the Job/People/Organization framework.

Chapter 30

Conduct a Post-Mortem

"Don't lower your expectations to meet your performance. Raise your level of performance to meet your expectations. Expect the best of yourself, and then do what is necessary to make it a reality."

- Ralph Marston

(Note: I do realize the term "post-mortem" means "the examination and dissection of a dead body to determine cause of death." Don't take me too literally here. I really mean "discussion of an event after it has occurred.")

LET'S FACE IT, you're going to have good interviews and not-so-good interviews. Sometimes the words will flow out of your mouth like the best orator you know. Other times? Well, you'll feel like you should have stayed in bed that morning.

One of the best ways to improve your performance in upcoming interviews is to dissect how the past one just went. Think of how professional athletes and their coaches watch game film over and over. They are trying to figure out what worked well and what didn't in order to improve their performance in the next game. Since you don't have game film to watch, how can you conduct an effective post-mortem?

Here is a little scoring tool to evaluate your own performance. Now, I realize you're not exactly objective but try not to trick yourself into thinking you did well when maybe you didn't. You can use the comments section to note areas where you could do better next time.

Statement	Score 1 - 10	Comments
I felt confident during the introductions and icebreaker		
I made a good first impression		
I dressed appropriately for the setting		
I answered their questions fully		
I asked penetrating questions of them		
By the end of the interview, I had made every point I wanted to make		
My body language conveyed the messages I wanted conveyed		
I know what the next steps are		
My closing comments were suitable		
I sent a follow-up thank you note		
TOTAL SCORE		

BEFORE MOVING ON

1. Thinking about your last two or three interviews, complete this scoring sheet and give yourself a grade. Be honest, there's no sense in lying to yourself. How can you improve your performance in future interviews?

Ask Gerry

Q. Is it possible to convince an employer that I can do the job even if I don't have all the qualifications?

A. At this stage, you have nothing to lose, so why not? However, I would not waste time trying to explain to them, verbally, why you can do the job. You will likely come across as desperate. Instead, show them. Let me give you an example.

Years ago, I met a young environmental engineer, Brad, who had just come from an informational interview with an engineering firm. The firm was meeting him as a courtesy as they had no openings and Brad, being a relatively-recent graduate, had limited experience. Brad was thrilled after meeting them and said to me, "I know I can help them." I encouraged him to prove that by writing a business plan explaining specifically how he could add value to the firm. To his credit, he did that and over the following week, produced a 15-page plan that documented what he could do. Fortunately, the firm was willing to meet with him again. They listened to his case, read his plan, and lo and behold, decided to hire him in a junior engineering position.

So, if you feel you have strong case, I would encourage you to do as Brad did.

Chapter 31

Always Send a Thank-You Note

"Take time to be kind and to say thank you."

\- Zig Ziglar

WHEN HUNTING FOR a job you need to find ways to stand out from the crowd. There is no sense in trying to blend in and be part of the scenery. You need to be different, hopefully in a positive way, so that employers will remember you.

One obvious way to give yourself a leg-up on your competition is to write a simple thank-you letter following the interview. I've never been able to figure this out but almost no one writes a thank-you letter. For some unknown reason, most people skip this really important part of the job-hunting process. Even Richard Bolles, author of *What Color is your Parachute* says he thinks it is the "most overlooked step in the entire job-hunting process."

So why is the thank-you letter so important?

Reason #1: It gives you an occasion to express gratitude for being given the opportunity to meet with the employer. In the business world, being polite and courteous still goes a long way. At the risk of sounding like my mother, it's just good manners.

Reason #2: Sending a "thank you" also gives you the chance to highlight key points about your background that are relevant to the job and to summarize why you are a good candidate. Take a look at the example I have used at the end of this chapter to see what I mean.

Reason #3: It also gives you the opportunity to point out any things that you may have forgotten to say during the interview. How many times does that happen? You leave an interview and say to yourself, "Darn, I forgot to tell them about ..." By then it's too late. You can't walk back into the interview room. A well-written thank-you letter gives you another chance to mention that significant point to them.

Reason #4: It helps the employer remember who you are. Sometimes employers will interview six or seven candidates (or even more) in one day. If you've ever been on the other side of that table (as I have many times) and interviewed that many people at once, you will appreciate how difficult it is to remember whether you liked earlier candidates or not. By stating something in your letter that was discussed in the interview, you will help the employer recall who you are.

Reason #5: Even if you've decided you don't want that job, it leaves the door open to future opportunities. It is good practice to maintain favourable relations with everybody you meet in the job search process. You never know when another (better) opportunity may arise with that company that might interest you or whether they could recommend you to another company.

When to Write a Thank-You Letter?

I think it's a good idea to wait a day or so before sending the thank-you note. You want to leave the employer with the impression that you have gone away and reflected on the discussion. You don't want to come across as impulsive.

I remember early in my recruiting career, I finished an interview with a candidate. We shook hands, he said thank you and proceeded down the hall and exited the building. About five minutes later, I too walked down the hall to head out for lunch. As I was going past our front desk, our receptionist passed me an envelope. I asked what it was. She said the fellow who I had just interviewed left this thank-you note on his way out.

I presume what happened was that he had read somewhere that you should always submit a thank-you letter. So, he took this literally and had one prepared in advance. That said nothing more to me than he had "read the book." The rest of his letter was entirely wasted.

What form should the letter take?

I keep saying "letter" throughout this chapter implying of course that it be a hand-written note. Actually, a traditional thank-you letter (or card) sent by regular mail is not such a bad idea. Since almost no one does this, your letter should stand out, however, email is a perfectly fine way of communicating your thanks to the employer. A sample thank you email letter is shown below.

Once you send the letter, plan a follow-up call about five to seven working days later. When making the call, you are not necessarily seeking a final decision. Rather, your call is an ongoing expression of interest, a demonstration of your willingness to initiate and one more chance to keep your name in front of the decision-makers.

Sample Thank-You Note

Here is a thank you email I received from a candidate the day after I interviewed her. I have edited it slightly to protect her identity and our client. Note how she links her experiences and skill set to our client's needs.

> Dear Mr. Walsh,
>
> Thank you for the interview yesterday. It was a pleasure speaking with you.
>
> I would like to restate my keen interest in the Executive Director position. I have had similar responsibilities as those mentioned in the job description - strategic planning, operations, team management, financial management, project management, event planning, logistics, etc. However, I wanted to elaborate on three areas which you indicated were of great importance:
>
> Relationship building - The core responsibility of my current role is relationship building. Since we work with local partners, we must build relationships with our partners at all levels as well as coordinate with the other humanitarian organizations present in the country. We also accompany our local partners to remote communities in order to engage community leaders, participate in needs assessments, and to monitor activities with community members.
>
> Human resources - I wanted to reinforce that I have had to manage small teams of people, both local staff and a team of international delegates. This includes being part of hiring process, doing performance reviews, and having to deal with difficult HR situations. I recognize a need for more experience in this area and am now taking an online course in leadership and management.
>
> Fundraising - In addition to writing many successful funding proposals and documenting stories for the marketing department, I have supported

our local partners in strengthening their capacities in resource mobilization, which is a broader concept that includes fundraising, accountability, and corporate partnerships. I have learned a lot on this topic that can be applied to the position in order to diversify the revenue sources for your client.

Finally, I would like to emphasize that I also offer motivation, dedication and creativity. I have many ideas of how I could apply my experience to innovate, market and diversify income for this organization. I would be very excited to have the opportunity to put these ideas into action.

Again, thank you for the opportunity and I look forward to a favourable reply with respect to being a part of the next step in this process.

Chapter 32

So, You Didn't Get The Job

"I've failed over and over and over again. And that is why I succeed."

- Michael Jordan

ONE OF THE parts of my job as an executive recruiter I like the least is calling candidates to tell them they did not get the job. No one likes delivering bad news, me included, but it is a necessary part of the process. Plus, I do know it is better to be straight-forward and let people know as soon as possible that they are not in the running any more. Most people prefer to know they did not get the job rather than hearing nothing at all, which unfortunately is the case more often than it should be.

How to handle rejection after an interview

I understand that finding out you did not get the job can be very disappointing particularly if it was a job you really wanted. If you've been looking for a job for a long time and received several rejections, the news can be even more disheartening. Most people will tell you to "accept it and move on" which is the right thing but much easier said than done. Here are a few thoughts and suggestions that might help you through this difficult phase:

Share your disappointment with a friend

The first step in getting over job rejection is to share your disappointment, frustration or anger with a friend or someone you feel confident sharing your emotions with. Even though it may feel like the last thing you feel like doing, heading out to the gym or out for a run is also one of the most effective ways to get rid of your frustrations.

Throughout this phase, I encourage you to acknowledge that the probability of getting any one job is low. That's because the competition is usually stiff with many talented people applying. Remember, only one person gets the job.

Analyze your performance during the interview process

If you can, try to obtain constructive feedback from the interviewers or recruiter. For example, not long ago, in response to a candidate asking, I told her that she might consider not relying on her notes too much as she came across as a bit scripted and not spontaneous enough. She appreciated that feedback and said she would adapt in future interviews.

I suggested to another candidate that he give fewer examples from his volunteer work and more from his paid work experience. I felt this would have been more effective in demonstrating his skills. He understood how this could improve his job interview performance in the future.

Often an employer will not give feedback but that shouldn't stop you from doing a critical self-analysis to determine if there is anything about your answers, dress, impression or questions that you could have done differently.

Also, don't eliminate the possibility that perhaps you did everything perfectly: that you performed to the best of your ability; demonstrated all your competencies and skills; and made a favourable impression. There was nothing more you could have done. It was just that there was a better qualified candidate who got the job.

Do not react in a negative way

When someone does provide feedback, even if you disagree, always accept the information with an open mind. Thank the person for providing it and never, ever react angrily or start to argue. They will not change their mind. It will come across as immature and unprofessional and almost certainly burn any bridges with that employer.

Here is an example of an appropriate email I received from a candidate after advising her she was not getting the job. Note the level of professionalism she displays:

Dear Gerry,

I really appreciate your call and the feedback you provided me. While I was obviously disappointed that I was not selected, I am confident they have chosen the right candidate for the job. Please do keep my resume on file in case you find a good match for me in the future. It was a pleasure meeting you.

Best regards,

[Name withheld]

Network with the interviewer

If you make a positive impression on the interviewer, even if you didn't get the job, she might be able to help you with your job search. Connect with them on LinkedIn and follow them on Twitter. And stay in touch with them via the occasional email. Who knows? Maybe the person they hired will not work out or perhaps another opening will arise.

Accept it and move on

Don't carry interview baggage with you. It will simply paralyze you and prevent you from being at the top of your game in future interviews. Instead, keep your momentum going by approaching new opportunities with enthusiasm and rigour. I believe there is the right job out there for everybody. Just keep at it until you find the right one for you.

Section Five

The Offer

"I walk away from anyone who is unduly focused on vacation and compensation. It's a sign of potential trouble. No matter how talented you are ... you'll never work out here."

- Blake Mycoskie, author, philanthropist, and founder of Toms Shoes

Chapter 33

The Anatomy of a Job Offer

"If you pick the right people and give them the opportunity to spread their wings and put compensation as a carrier behind it, you almost don't have to manage them."

- Jack Welch

THE JOB OFFER is a formal written document provided by an employer to a candidate, which outlines everything you will need to know about your future employment. It is a very important document because once accepted by you it governs the entire employment relationship you will have with this employer.

Let's dissect a job offer here so you will understand each of its components and what you can expect. This is an offer that was presented to a candidate for Executive Director of a professional association. While the content of the offer is taken from an actual job offer, the names of the association and candidate are changed. My comments, explaining what each section means for you, are presented beneath each relevant clause.

Opening:
On behalf of the Board of Directors of the Ontario Road Runners Association ("ORRA"), I am pleased to convey this letter of offer to you subject to the following terms and conditions:

Title:
Executive Director

Reporting to:
Board of Directors through the Chair

Responsibilities:
Per job description attached

What does this mean?

Your immediate reporting relationship should be identified here. It is always best if the offer refers to positions or titles (such as "Chair") rather than using the person's name as that person will change over time.

Since this letter of employment, once signed, forms a contract between you and the employer, it is essential that your duties and responsibilities be listed here or enclosed as an attachment.

Salary:
Your salary will be $110,000 per annum. This salary will be reviewed annually, and any increases will be determined based on an annual performance review with the Board of Directors, and subject to budgetary constraints.

What does this mean?

In addition to identifying your starting salary, you should ensure that the basis upon which salary reviews will take place are clearly identified. Often this point is omitted from job offers, not by design, but just due to oversight. Although this example suggests that salary increases are linked to the performance review, it is not uncommon in many organizations for the salary reviews and performance reviews to be uncoupled and completed at separate times of the year.

Benefits:
You are eligible to participate in the group benefits plan made available to all employees of ORRA, in accordance with the terms and conditions of the plan. Coverage includes life insurance, accidental death and dismemberment, long-term disability, health and dental. Details of this plan can be provided to you. The standard waiting period to join the plan is three (3) months.

What does this mean?

This is standard wording that says you can participate in the plan, like all other employees. The phrase "in accordance with the terms and conditions of the plan" is there to allow for changes in the plan over time. In most cases, your potential employer has an executive summary of the plan details and should provide this to you. You should review it carefully, as it forms part of your total compensation. In many cases, the cost sharing of premiums for coverage is noted in the offer. This is usually 50/50, meaning the employer and employee each share the cost equally. Waiting periods are standard in group policies although the employer can request waiver of this restriction from the insurance provider. Unless you have comparable coverage elsewhere, you should seek waiver. Otherwise you will be left without coverage for three months.

Pension:

You are eligible to participate in ORRA's RRSP pension plan in accordance with the terms and condition of the plan. Under this plan, ORRA will match your contributions to a self-directed plan of your choice to a maximum of 5% of your salary. You are eligible for this plan after one year of employment.

What does this mean?

Pension plans fall into one of two categories: defined-benefit (where the benefit you receive is identified in advance, such as 2% times your years of service) or defined-contribution (where the amount you contribute is defined in advance but the amount you receive is not). The example shown is a matching, defined contribution. Note that if you only contribute 3% of your salary to this plan, the employer will only contribute 3%. So, there is a clear incentive for you to contribute at the maximum level. When you leave this employer, at retirement or before, you will take both the employer's share and your share with you.

Travel:

Any work-related travel and expenses incurred in the ordinary course of ORRA business will be reimbursed in accordance with regular staff policy.

What does this mean?

This just simply clarifies that should you have to travel or entertain for business-related purposes, you are eligible for, and must comply with, the company's policies.

Vacation:

You are entitled to the equivalent of three (3) weeks' vacation per annum, earned at rate of 1.25 days per month of employment. In accordance with policy, this vacation entitlement will increase to four (4) weeks per annum after five (5) years of employment. It is expected that you will use your vacation entitlement in the year in which it is earned, although up to five (5) days may be carried over to the following year with approval.

What does this mean?

Everybody is entitled to time off and you should be clear in the beginning how your vacation is calculated so there are no misunderstandings. This example is pretty clear in describing how vacation entitlement is determined. If the job requires evening or weekend work, you should inquire if this is compensated as extra pay or time off in lieu, or is it just expected that you will work those additional hours without further compensation.

Confidentiality:

During your employment with ORRA, you will be exposed to confidential information that is not generally known outside ORRA. During and following the term of your employment, you agree to not disclose any secret or confidential information or information which in good faith and in good conscience ought to be treated as confidential, which becomes known to you in the course of your employment with ORRA.

What does this mean?

This is a standard confidentiality clause that many organizations require for all employees. Although the wording may differ among companies, essentially this clause says that things you learn about the company, such as client lists, pricing information, and trade secrets, cannot be disclosed to others while you are employed there and even after you leave.

Exclusivity:

Your sole and exclusive employment shall be as Executive Director of the Ontario Road Runners Association. In this capacity, you shall faithfully serve ORRA and use your best efforts to promote the interests of ORRA. Notwithstanding the foregoing, during the term of your employment with ORRA, should you wish to enter into a service contract with a third party, or engage in an ownership capacity, either directly or indirectly, with any private business, you shall first obtain written approval of the Board of Directors.

What does this mean?

For senior positions in particular, an exclusivity clause is not uncommon. In effect, this says that you will devote all your time and attention to the organization. It also guards against potential conflicts of interest arising by requiring the Board's consent for involvement in any outside interests. Note that it does not say you cannot have outside interests. It is only saying Board consent is required first.

Termination:

Your employment as Executive Director may be terminated in the following manner in the specified circumstances:

a) You may terminate your employment at any time, for any reason, on giving three (3) months' written notice to the Board of Directors.

b) ORRA may terminate your employment for just cause without notice or payment in lieu of notice.

c) ORRA may terminate your employment <u>without just cause</u> by providing working notice, or pay in lieu of notice, equal to one (1) month of salary for each full year of employment as Executive Director, to a maximum of six (6) months.

In the case of a part-year of service, the above amount shall be calculated on a pro-rated basis by week. In no case, shall the termination pay exceed six (6) months.

Should termination under clause (c) occur, ORRA in its sole discretion will determine whether to provide you with working notice or pay in lieu of notice or a combination of both. If ORRA elects to provide you pay in lieu of notice it may, in its sole discretion pay you your pay in lieu of notice by way of a lump-sum payment, in which case any benefits coverage and pension contributions will cease upon termination. Alternatively, ORRA may elect to provide your pay in lieu of notice by way of salary continuation in which case benefit coverage (with the exception of long-term disability) will continue until the conclusion of your salary continuance.

What does this mean?

It may seem strange to speak about termination at time of hire but it is in everyone's best interests, including yours, to clearly define what will happen if the employment relationship falls apart and you are facing termination. This example covers it fully.

Clause (a) states what your obligations are if you decide unilaterally to leave the organization. Three months, as shown here, is fairly long and you should attempt to negotiate this downward if possible. The reason a shorter period is better for you is that if you are moving to another job your future employer may not want to wait three months for you to start work. The bottom line is that while this clause is difficult to enforce, it is a moral commitment on your part. Failing to live up to its terms could result in "burning a bridge" with this employer.

Clause (b) deals with termination for "just cause." Just cause is defined in law and generally means that "an employee has been guilty of serious misconduct, habitual neglect of duty, incompetence, or conduct incompatible with his duties, or prejudicial to the employer's business, or ... guilty of willful disobedience to the employer's orders in a matter of substance." Actions like theft, fraud, gross misconduct, or insubordination usually fall within this definition. If the employer can prove that you were fired for just cause, you receive no severance pay.

Clause (c) is the one most commonly applied. While an employer may want to dismiss someone for just cause, that is much harder to prove and usually involves going through the courts. So they usually end up paying severance, which is always best to determine in advance. In our example, the amount paid is equal to one month's salary per full year of service. The latter part of clause (c) details the payment options, either as a lump-sum payment or a salary continuation for the severance period. From your point of view, there is no absolute best way to receive the money. Some people prefer to take the money and move on. Others want the security of regular pay and benefits while they seek another job. There are tax implications for either situation, therefore you should seek professional advice before making a decision.

Conditions:
This offer of employment is subject to confirmation of your academic and professional qualifications, and receipt of satisfactory professional references.

What does this mean?
In some instances a job offer is made before all the conditions of employment have been met. In this example, the company wants to receive copies of academic and professional credentials, plus obtain satisfactory references. You should note that the offer is not legally binding until all these conditions have been met. It would be advisable to not resign your current job until the company has confirmed to you that these conditions have been satisfied.

Acceptance:

I acknowledge that:

a) I have had sufficient time to thoroughly review this Offer of Employment as Executive Director of the Ontario Road Runners Association;
b) I understand the terms of this Offer of Employment and the obligations hereunder;
c) I have been given an opportunity to obtain independent legal advice concerning the interpretation and effect of this Offer of Employment Agreement; and
d) I accept this Offer of Employment on the terms and conditions set out.

Signed,

Your Name / Date

What does this mean?
Be careful. Make absolutely certain that you understand what this document says and all the implications of each section. That's because once you sign it, it becomes the official employment contract between you and your new employer.

Chapter 34

Use Your Head,
Not Your Heart

**"A wise man should have money in his head,
but not in his heart."**

- Jonathan Swift

EARLY IN MY recruiting career, I learned the importance of having a formal way for evaluating job offers.

I was conducting a search for a Marketing Analyst for a large employer. The company was offering a salary in the $60,000 range and there was substantial upward potential within their organization. The company was also a big promoter of professional development and encouraged all their employees to improve their skills through training.

One of the candidates I interviewed and ultimately presented to the company was Sam (not his real name). When I first interviewed Sam to learn about his experience and qualifications, he told me he was interested in moving from a small town, where he then lived, to the city where my client was located which was where his fiancée lived. He also indicated that his salary expectations were in the $50,000 - $55,000 range.

When I probed further about his other career expectations and aspirations, here's what I learned:

- Since he was still relatively early in his career, he wanted to work for a company that offered plenty of room for advancement.
- He wanted the work to be challenging and meaningful, not routine and boring.
- He wanted his next employer to be one that valued professional development and that would be willing to invest in its employees through

training. As he noted, many companies say that employees are their greatest asset yet do nothing to affirm that statement.

- Sam also hoped that his bosses and co-workers would be nice people and fun to work with, and that work environment was very important to him. He noted as well that he valued work/life balance and ideally would like four weeks' vacation, which is what he now received at his much-smaller employer.

- Finally, he noted that job security would soon become important to him as he and his fiancée planned to marry soon and eventually have a family.

Here's what happened.

After a series of interviews during which Sam met most of the senior management team and many of his potential co-workers, our client decided to make an offer to Sam. The offer was for $60,000 (remember Sam originally wanted $50,000 - $55,000) and in addition they would give him a $5,000 moving allowance, something Sam was not expecting. He had fully expected to pay for his own relocation.

They offered a professional development allowance of $1,500 per year and spoke of areas in which he could take training that would position him well for future promotions in the company.

Sam really liked all the people he met and knew from their description of the work that he would find it challenging and fun. It looked like the perfect opportunity for Sam, perhaps even better!

Except for one thing: They offered Sam three weeks' vacation; Sam wanted four weeks.

When he raised this concern with them, they explained that there was really no flexibility on vacation because there were many other employees at Sam's level who only received three weeks. They felt that making an exception for him could damage morale among other staff and possibly cause resentment toward Sam. Their hands were tied, they explained.

Sadly, Sam turned down the offer because of the vacation issue. Even though he was getting everything he wanted (and more) in every other aspect of the offer, the fact that he was not getting the amount of vacation he wanted became his primary focus and his number one reason for declining the job.

How could this possibly happen, you say?

It's because in the absence of a structured decision-making framework, you have no capacity for making an informed, well-thought-out decision. Therefore, items that for many people would be seventh or eighth on their list of priorities (like length of vacation) all of a sudden become number one!

In this case, Sam could not see clearly that his needs (well, at least most of them) were being met. Instead, he let his emotions cloud his thinking in what should really be a business decision.

How to build a decision framework

Sam would have been better served if he had developed a decision-making framework before starting his search. In this framework, he could list the criteria that are important to him in a job and assign relative weightings (or rankings) to each one.

Let's work through this process together using Sam's situation as an example.

The first step is to identify the top ten factors that are most important to you in a job. Based on my professional experience, it seems to me that, on average, there are about ten items that matter to most people in career selection. However if you have more than ten (or fewer than ten), you can still benefit from this analysis.

Think back to chapter seven where you described what you want from your work. At that time, you described them but did not rank them. Here is where you will rank them. Start by checking off the ones that are on your "most important" list.

___ Compensation
___ Benefits
___ Vacation
___ Physical location
___ Nice workspace
___ Industry
___ Company size
___ Job security
___ Good boss that I respect
___ Nice people to work with
___ Status
___ Prestigious title
___ Personal and professional growth

___ Meaningful work
___ Opportunity for advancement
___ Recognition and achievement
___ Culture
___ Other _____
___ Other _____
___ Other _____

Once you have your 10 factors selected, you will then begin step two: the process of grouping and then ranking your choices. I would recommend that you group your choices into three categories:

Category 1: Absolutely essential that I have these in a job;
Category 2: Very important to me but not absolutely essential; and
Category 3: Of lesser importance, but still nice to have.

Based on what we know about Sam's intentions, here is how he might have grouped and ranked his criteria:

Absolutely essential that Sam has these in a job:
1. Location
2. Opportunity for advancement
3. Challenging work

Very important to Sam but not absolutely essential:
4. Salary and benefits
5. Professional development
6. Nice people to work with

Of lesser importance to Sam, but still nice to have:
7. Company size
8. Work environment
9. Vacation
10. Job security

Once your list is developed, then you must evaluate each item. In other words, compare the actual job offer against your set of most important items. This is step three. A simple "Not Met", "Met" or "Exceeded" framework is helpful. Here is how Sam might have done it.

Rank	Factor	Not Met	Met	Exceeded
1	Location		x	
2	Opportunity for promotion		x	
3	Challenging work		x	
4	Salary and benefits			x
5	Professional development		x	
6	Nice people to work with			x
7	Company size		x	
8	Work environment		x	
9	Vacation	X		
10	Job security		x	

While there is no actual scoring system built into this process that gives you a definitive accept or decline answer, this matrix demonstrates that out of Sam's top 10 items seven have been met and two others were even exceeded. Only one (vacation) was not met. It is safe to assume that most would accept a job with the above profile.

If you're more comfortable using "numbers" to quantify your decision, rather relying on a qualitative analysis, here is an alternative way to do that:

1. Weight your decision criteria by dividing 100 points among them;
2. Score how the offer meets each criteria on a 1 – 10 scale;
3. Calculate the weighted average total score for the offer.

Using this approach, here is how Sam might have evaluated his offer. (Note: I am using my own judgment on the weightings.)

Rank	Factor	Weight	1 – 10	Weighted Average
1	Location	20	10/10	20.0
2	Opportunity for advancement	15	8/10	12.0
3	Challenging work	15	8/10	12.0
4	Salary and benefits	10	10/10	10.0
5	Professional development	8	10/10	8.0
6	Nice people to work with	8	9/10	7.2
7	Company size	7	7/10	4.9
8	Work environment	7	7/10	4.9
9	Vacation	6	4/10	2.4
10	Job security	4	7/10	2.8
	Total	**100**		**83.2**

This method is useful if you happen to be lucky enough to have two job offers at the same time, as it is a great way to compare one offer against the other.

Or, if you are currently employed and not sure if you want to leave your job to accept another one, you can rate your current job against the job offer to determine if it makes sense to accept. If the new offer scores higher, then you accept that one. If not, stay where you are.

Remember, if you're really going to use your head and not your heart when evaluating job offers, you must have three things:

a.   A list of what is important to you in a job;
b.   A way of ranking them from most important to least important;
c.   A way of evaluating or scoring them.

If you have these in place and can evaluate them objectively, I am confident you will make the right decision for yourself.

What happened to Sam?

About a week after Sam declined the offer, he came to the realization that he had made a mistake. That in fact, vacation should not have been so high on his list of priorities that it should, alone, have caused him to turn down the offer. After all, his other expectations were met.

So, he went back to the employer, explained his rationale, and said that if he was re-offered the job, with the same terms, he would accept it. But regrettably it was too late for Sam. The number two candidate had been offered the job after Sam declined and she had accepted.

Don't Get Confused by Flattery

There's an old fable about the fox and the crow that could have some meaning for you when evaluating job offers.

In the fable the crow finds a piece of cheese and flies to a branch to eat it. From below, the fox sees her eating the cheese and decides he wants it for himself. So, he starts to flatter her, telling her how pretty she is and wondering (out loud) if her singing voice is as beautiful as she is.

The crow, loving the flattery, decides to sing by letting out a caw. As expected, the cheese falls out of her mouth to the ground below and the sly fox happily devours it.

The moral of the story is: don't listen to flattery as it will cloud your judgment. How is this relevant to job offers? As you advance through the interviewing process and eventually reach the stage where the company makes you an offer (but before you accept), they might begin the process of introducing you to senior executives or taking you out for lunch, dinner or drinks. By this point they have decided they want you to join their organization and believe that this step of "wining and dining you" (as I like to refer to it) might help convince you to say yes. From your perspective, these types of meetings could be helpful. So don't decline them as they could shed more light on the company and help with your decision.

But be aware that this is a subtle form of flattery. Just be cautious that you don't lose your judgment.

Chapter 35

Determine What
You Are Worth

"Do your job and demand your compensation - but in that order."

- Cary Grant

MOST PEOPLE HAVE a pretty good idea what they are worth based on their experience, education, qualifications. But in some instances, such as when you are moving to another part of the country or perhaps hitting the job market after many years working for a single employer, your current pay level may not be relevant anymore.

If you want to check this against the "market" there are a few places where you can go. Note that some of these are free and others will cost you money.

One is called *Salary Wizard Canada* run by Monster.ca. It is a free online resource that provides salary information by region for more than 50 job categories. For each position, the site provides a brief job profile plus details about pay and bonuses. What it doesn't tell you is how they arrived at the data, including the sample size they used. *Payscale.com* and *Salary.com* are two alternate sites that work the same way as Salary Wizard.

In Canada, the Labour Market Information Service available through Service Canada (servicecanada.gc.ca) will help you find "information about occupations and labour market trends and outlooks, including skill or labour shortages and surpluses, and statistics on unemployment …"

The site *workingincanada.gc.ca* gives valuable salary and job-related information on a local and provincial level. The site called *Living in Canada* (livingin-Canada.ca) is a good source of hourly wage rates for those occupations that usually pay by the hour, such as trades and service-related jobs. The only fault with this site is that data is limited to only a few cities in Canada and not for the whole country.

There are thousands of professional and industry associations in Canada, representing everyone from doctors to truckers. A number of these associations publish annual salary surveys and guides for their members. If you are a member of that group, you may get it for free. If you're not, you can usually obtain the information for a fee.

To get a master list of "associations in Canada" simply do an online search for those words and you'll be directed to a series of sites that will give you give you the listings. Remember, too, that professional bodies in Canada (accountants, engineers, lawyers, etc.) are actually governed provincially, not nationally, although there is usually an umbrella national organization. Salary data might be kept with the provincial body if you can't find anything on the national site, so don't forget to check there too.

Likewise, for salary information in the not-for-profit sector, you might check *Charity Village,* a website and job site for that sector.

You can also get solid advice on going rates from recruiters who will have a lot of experience negotiating salaries. And don't overlook obvious sources, such as simply asking people who work in the field for salary guidance on the type of position you are seeking.

BEFORE MOVING ON

1. Although it is not necessary to arrive at a definitive number at this stage, it is always wise to have a good idea of your "market value" before embarking on your job search. Take some time to do research and speak to people "in the know." It is better to be informed now rather than waiting until you receive an offer.

Chapter 36

Negotiate Like a Pro

"During a negotiation, it would be wise not to take anything personally. If you leave personalities out of it, you will be able to see opportunities more objectively."

- Brian Koslow

THERE ARE A few rules of thumb you should know about before starting the salary negotiation process. A number of these rules fall under the "etiquette" category while others are just plain "common sense." If you manage this process well and professionally, you should end up with the best possible outcome for you.

Rule #1
Always let the employer bring up the salary question first

Nothing turns off an employer quicker than a candidate asking about salary too early in the process. Arguably, there is merit in raising this question early so no one wastes time if the gap is too large between what the employer wants to pay and what the candidate wants to receive. However this is one of the protocols that is so engrained in the hiring process that if a candidate violates it, it is almost considered rude. So be patient. It will come up eventually, assuming the employer is interested in you, of course.

Rule #2
The best time to negotiate salary is before you start with a new employer

This is because the opportunity cost of receiving a lower-than-hoped-for salary is so high over the course of your career. Why is that? Take, for example, two individuals (Mike and Lisa), each 35 years old and starting new jobs. Mike starts at a salary of $60,000. Lisa is making slightly higher at $65,000. Assuming each of their salaries increase by 3% annually from age 35 to when they retire at age

65, over those 30 years Mike will have earned $2,854,000 while Lisa will have earned $3,092,000. That's a difference of $238,000!

	Mike	**Lisa**
Starting salary	$60,000	$65,000
Age now	35	35
Planned retirement age	65	65
Average salary increase per year	3%	3%
Total earnings from age 35 to 65	$2,854,000	$3,092,000

This shows you that the compounding effect of successful salary negotiation can be sizeable. While the difference between $60,000 and $65,000 might not seem like much at the start, over the lifespan of your career it becomes a meaningful amount. That is why you should always negotiate for as much as you can (without offending anyone) before you start with an employer.

Rule #3
Avoid being the first to quote a definitive salary amount

One of the core principles of successful negotiation is to understand that the party that puts a number on the table first is automatically at a disadvantage. That's because the other person now knows what your threshold is.

Say you are looking at buying a used car. You find one on a used car site. You take it for test drive and discover you like it. The seller says, "Make me an offer." If you take the bait and offer, say, $12,000, that now anchors the negotiation. The seller knows that your minimum price is $12,000 and in all likelihood you would go higher.

What if it had gone the other way though? When the seller invited you to make him an offer, instead of offering $12,000 right away, you said, "Well, what do you want for it? How much are you willing to sell it for?" The ball has now been volleyed back to the seller. If he then says, "I think it's worth $11,000." Well, you've just saved yourself at least $1,000.

The same basic rules of negotiation apply to salary negotiation. If an employer asks, "What are your salary expectations?" try to toss it back to him by asking, "I am interested in this role. Has a salary range been set?"

A word of caution though: if this back and forth process goes on too long, you can turn off the employer. If he keeps pressing for your expectations, you are going to have to state them.

Rule #4
Never accept an offer on the spot

Even if the offer comes in at more than you wanted (which is rare), you should never sign on the dotted line immediately. If you do, you run the risk of coming across as impulsive and careless. An offer is an important document because it guides your employment tenure with that employer. It is the employment contract between you and your employer. So, even if the employer wants an answer quickly (which is common), you can certainly take it overnight and think about it. In fact, most employers will allow anywhere up to seven days for you to make a decision.

Rule #5
There is usually some room for negotiation but probably not much

For most junior and mid-level jobs, as well as many senior level jobs, I would say there is room to negotiate for about 5% to 10% more than what was offered. Here are a few thoughts to keep in mind.

Contrary to what some candidates think, most employers are not trying to take advantage of you by giving you a low-ball offer. Unless your prospective employer is unscrupulous, you can assume that the offer is within a reasonable range of what they feel the job is worth (or what they can afford to pay.) So while you might be able to move the salary up a notch or two, it is probably no more than the 5% - 10% range.

In some cases, there is simply no room to negotiate due to financial restrictions. For example, in some provinces in Canada, the salaries of administrators of publicly funded nursing homes are paid a set amount for each bed in the home. This amount is determined by the provincial government and there is simply no flexibility, no matter how strong the candidate. Small, not-for-profit organizations also operate with very tight budgets and often cannot afford to pay more than the stated salary.

This does not mean, however, that you shouldn't ask for more. As long as you have built an atmosphere of mutual trust throughout the interview process, you have nothing to lose and everything to gain by asking what the employer can do to get you closer to your targeted salary. If they cannot move on salary, they might be willing to give you more vacation or some other non-cash form of compensation. Either way, employers are almost always flexible on some part of the offer.

Ask Gerry

Q. Last week, I accepted a job offer with a new employer which I had planned to start in three weeks. I have now just received an offer from another company. This was the offer I really wanted to get. The money is better and I like the people more. How would you recommend I handle this situation?

A. Without a doubt, this is an awkward situation you find yourself in although you are not the first person who has faced it. Unfortunately there is no clear-cut answer on what to do here. What you are balancing is a moral obligation to the first employer who offered you the job in good faith (which you accepted) against the practical reality of the second offer, which is a better one for you in most respects, including money. You will have to judge whether it is better for you to "stick to your word" and keep with the first offer or go with the one you have determined is better for you.

If you do decide to reject the first offer, the classy way to do it would be to meet with the employer in person, carefully explaining what has happened and why you changed your mind. It would also be helpful if you were able to offer some sort of solution to the problem you helped create, such as mentioning someone else who might be good for the job.

Rule #6
Think about "total" compensation not just base salary

I have seen too many salary negotiations get off track because all of the focus is on base salary only. What is left out of the discussion is the overall value of benefits, pensions, memberships, parking and other perks.

Take a look at an actual job offer (on the following pages) made to a candidate at a base salary level of $52,500. Here is how "total" compensation should be calculated for that offer:

Base salary	$52,500
Benefits based on single enrollment (approx.)	1,800
Pension contribution	2,625
Professional development allowance	1,600
Wellness plan	200
Parking	1,200
Value of compensation plan	**$59,925**

An offer with a base salary of $52,500 is actually worth at least $59,925. And this does not take into account the potential to earn a bonus of up to 20% of base salary. If things go well, that could be worth over $10,000 more!

———————

This is an actual job offer made to a candidate, although her name and that of the employer have been changed.

Ms. Jill Zephyr
208-1234 Flying Cloud Street
Town of Ladysmith, BC V9G 1A2

Dear Jill,

Thank you very much for taking the time to meet with us regarding our search for a new team member. We were very impressed with your resume, professionalism and enthusiasm and feel there is a good match between your goals and the position with our company. I am pleased to be able to make you an offer as *Accounting Manager* with Smarty Pants Inc.

- Your proposed start date will be February 25, 2013 in accordance with your availability. Please let us know if you need an adjustment to the dates.

- Your annual starting base salary will be $52,500. Salary reviews are done annually for all employees in February of each year, with performance reviews every trimester.

- Employee benefits will become effective one month after your start date with the company. You will be provided two times your salary in basic life insurance, and an excellent comprehensive medical, dental, and long-term disability plan. All costs of the benefits package are paid 100% by the company with the exception of long-term disability (LTD). By having you pay the costs for LTD, this ensures that if LTD benefits are required they would come to you on a tax-free basis. The total benefits paid by the company on behalf of employees is an important addition to the overall compensation package as many companies ask that their employees share in the premium contributions.

- The company has an annual performance bonus, which can total up to 20% of your base salary (depending on company performance and your own contribution to company operations.) This bonus is awarded annually in February and becomes available after one year with the company.

- The company has a Wellness Plan designed to enhance or contribute to employees' wellness and/or level of fitness. Funding is made available to each employee to cover 50% of the expense up to $200 a year for the pursuit of wellness or fitness. Eligibility begins after the first year of employment.

- The company will contribute 5% of your base salary to a self-directed pension plan of your choice.

- The company's Professional Development Account will be available for your use for professional development activities (e.g. courses, conferences, resources) pending approval from your manager. This amount would be in addition to your annual salary and would become available beginning in January of each year. The allowance is calculated using an amount equivalent to 3% of your base salary up to $30,000, plus 2% of your base salary over $30,000. Employees with one year of service are eligible for this allocation.

- The company approaches every employment relationship confident that both parties will work together in a positive and fulfilling way. To the benefit of both parties, the position is subject to a six-month probationary period from start date.

- Vacation allocation is calculated at 1.25 days per month (15 business days per year.) The vacation year is based on the calendar year. Any vacation unused by year-end can be rolled over for 60 days pending arrangements with your manager. As a benefit to employees, annual vacation allocation can be taken in advance of days earned during the course of the year with approval. If an employee were to leave before earning vacation used, this would be reconciled in the final pay.

- Additional holidays are occasionally offered to staff as a benefit. We typically offer summer time days which is an additional half-day before the three long weekends starting July 1st. In addition, the company provides extra time at Christmas when the office will be closed.

- Parking is also available to employees at no charge.

Jill, if you have any questions at all or would like any clarification, please feel free to contact me. On accepting our offer, please sign and date both documents and return to me for your personnel and payroll file. We look forward to having you join our company as part of our team.

Sincerely,

SMARTY PANTS INC.

I.M. Smart
President and CEO

Chapter 37

Accept the Offer With Enthusiasm

"I am an ordinary person who has been blessed with extraordinary opportunities and experiences. Today is one of those experiences."

- Sonia Sotomayor

I'M A BIG believer in putting job offers in writing to avoid any misunderstanding down the road. Don't forget, at time of hire trust levels are high and everyone is looking forward to a wonderful employment relationship.

But like all relationships, things can sour. So, everyone (that means the employer and you) is best served if the offer is written because once accepted by you it governs the entire employment relationship you will have with your employer.

How to Respond to a Written Job Offer

In most cases, your potential employer will present you with a written job offer. Assuming it covers all the points you wanted and deals with your concerns satisfactorily, it is best to respond with a written acceptance that is well planned, well written, and professional. You've already made a positive first impression on the employer. Otherwise, they would not have offered you the job. Keep this positive impression going with a properly crafted acceptance letter.

Here is the framework that your letter should follow:

1. Include your employer's complete name, title, address and date, ensuring that everything is complete and spelled correctly. I know this sounds elementary but many people make errors with basic information. The best way to approach this is to take the information directly from the employer's business card or web site, and present the way they present it. If they're in

"Saskatchewan" they may spell this out in its entirety in the address. Or they may use "Sask" or "SK." Whatever they use, you should use.

2. Express your sincere thanks and appreciation for being offered the job, and tell them that you are pleased to accept their offer. (Note: it's important, from a legal perspective, to say "I accept.")

3. Confirm your start date, which is the effective date of your employment agreement and verify any other outstanding matters.

4. Close with another thank you and tell them you are looking forward to working with them.

Here's an example of an appropriate acceptance letter:

Sam Snowbird
President
Aerobatic Jets Inc.
228 Main Street North
Moose Jaw, SK S6H 3J8

Dear Mr. Snowbird,

Thank you for offering me the job of Sales Manager with Aerobatic Jets Inc. I am very pleased to accept this offer and look forward to starting with you on May 15, 2014.

As discussed, I will be in touch with your human resources department to complete the necessary paperwork and pick up the details of the benefits package.

Once again, I thank you for giving me this opportunity. I am very excited about working with you and the entire team at Aerobatic Jets and know I will be able to make a positive contribution to your company.

Sincerely,

Patrick Propeller

What to Do if The Offer is Verbal

Most employers will put the offer in writing if you ask. However, if for some reason, your potential employer only agrees to make the offer verbally, what you should do is write a detailed acceptance letter that outlines all the terms and conditions of the offer, as you understand them.

Here's an example of how to do that:

Ms. Annie Gables
Gables-by-the-Sea
4356 Grafton Street
Charlottetown, PE C1A 4B7

Dear Ms. Gables,

Thank you for offering me the position of Office Manager with Gables-by-the-Sea. So we are all clear, I would like to summarize my understanding of the terms of employment:

- My starting salary will be $67,500 per year and I will be eligible for an annual salary increase on the anniversary dates of my employment.
- I will be eligible for the company's standard health and life benefits after the normal 90-day waiting period.
- I will be entitled to three weeks' vacation, increasing to four weeks after five years of employment.
- The company will provide a laptop computer and cell phone for business use.
- My regular hours of work will be 8:30 am – 5:00 pm, Monday through Friday, although I understand some overtime may be required from time to time depending on work flow.

Please let me know if your understanding of these terms of employment differs from mine. If you are in agreement with these terms, I am pleased to accept your offer and am looking forward to starting on September 24th. Thank you again for giving me this wonderful opportunity.

Yours truly,

R.U. (Uberto) Clear

Ask Gerry

Q. I've accepted a new job and have given one month's notice to my current employer. Is there anything I should be doing with my new employer during this notice period?

A. Yes, I always think it is a good idea to keep in touch with your new employer while you finish out your employment with your current employer. There are plenty of things you can do. For example, why not invite your new boss out for lunch to discuss priorities? Or you could ask for company materials, such as business plans, annual reports or budgets, to help you prepare for beginning employment. As a minimum, you should offer to drop by the new office to get signed on to the benefits plan and meet some of your fellow workers. If they happen to invite you to a company event, like the annual picnic, make sure you attend. Small steps like these will demonstrate your enthusiasm for the new job and your eagerness to fit in.

Chapter 38

Decline the Offer
Without Burning Bridges

"Be careful the bridges you're willing to burn when trying to get ahead. You never know when you'll need a friend again."

- Britt Thelemann

THERE ARE LOADS of reasons why you might turn down a job offer even after you've been through a series of interviews, meetings and testing. However it can be awkward particularly since you've been signaling your interest in the job all along by continuing in the interview process.

One thing you want to avoid is leaving the employer with the impression that you're stringing them along. This does happen on occasion when an individual goes through the entire interview process solely for the purpose of extracting more money from their current employer. Or, I have seen some individuals go through the process for "practice" so they can beef up their interviewing skills.

Both those examples are clearly unethical and I would not recommend you adopt either one. But even if you were sincere, some employers may conclude (incorrectly) that was your motive all along. You must not leave them with that impression.

As with most things in life, the best approach when turning down a job offer is: tell the truth. And do it with tact, respect and professionalism.

There are many reasons why you might turn down an offer in the end. But these reasons usually revolve around one of three things: money, the work or the people at the company.

Take compensation, for example. Here's what often happens. Most companies state a salary range for the position. Say it is $70,000 to $90,000. You might proceed through the interview phase thinking that you could get an offer as high as $90,000, which might be your target range.

But here's the problem. Employers are most comfortable at (or below) the mid-point of a range. So say the offer is $77,000, a far cry from your target of $90,000. In this instance, it is thoughtful to say to the employer that you are hoping for a salary closer to the higher end of the range but that you understand their need to be closer to the mid-point. That shows empathy toward their position while at the same time re-states your salary objective.

It would be inappropriate to say that you were "offended" by their offer and believe that you are "worth" $90,000, as I have seen done. While this may be true, it is best to leave that unsaid!

There are also a few guidelines you should follow when declining an offer. Always try your best to make it personal by doing it in person or by phone. There is a great temptation to hide behind email particularly when doing difficult things.

But how you communicate says a lot about your character. So even though it is uncomfortable, I would suggest you call the hiring manager and explain your reason for declining. They will respect you a lot more for not taking the easy way out.

In this call, you should be clear (without offending anyone) why you are turning down the offer. If their salary offer is off-market with competing firms, it is better for them in the long run to know this as they will encounter recruitment and retention problems if this discrepancy is not fixed. Your feedback can help them.

However if the reason you are turning them down is because you found the personality of your potential boss to be repulsive, I would suggest you say diplomatically that you "did not feel the fit was right." It's okay to be a little less than honest in this case.

A couple of other rules to follow:

- Once you've decided to turn down the offer, let the employer know right away. Any delay might cause them to miss out on other potential candidates.
- If you know of anyone else who might be good for the job, mention this to the employer. You will come across as helping them solve their problems.

- As always, do this with sincerity and appreciation, even if they are initially disappointed in you. They will get over it. Don't forget, your main goal is to not burn any bridges with that employer and to keep the door open for future possibilities. While the fit might not be right for now that may change down the road.

Ask Gerry

Q. I was pleased to receive a job offer recently but after thinking about it for a few days, I decided to turn it down. When I spoke to the hiring manager and told her the news, she asked if I would be open to another offer. I told her "thanks" but that I had already made my decision. Afterward, I was uncomfortable with how I answered her question. Could I have done that differently?

A. If you are turning down the offer because of money alone, you should be receptive to another offer that raises the proposed salary. Or if the company cannot increase their offer for whatever reason, they may be able to offer you non-cash forms of compensation, such as a four-day work week or another week's vacation. In any event, you should be willing to review a better offer as this problem can be fixed quickly.

If it's the work itself that turns you off (such as doing repetitive tasks) you might ask if the job can be redesigned to give you more challenging work or broader responsibilities. Some companies do have the flexibility to modify jobs. If they are open to doing so, then ask them to define the changes and send you another offer with an updated job description attached.

Chapter 39

Quit With Class

**"Anyone can throw a temper tantrum and walk out of a job.
That's easy and any moron can do it."**

- Richard Lowe, Jr.

QUITTING YOUR JOB is not easy. Even if your new job offers you more pay, is closer to home, and offers greater career potential, it can be still difficult to leave your current employer.

But once you do decide that leaving your job is best, do it with class. Always take the high road by acting professionally and showing concern for the problems your resignation might create for your current employer.

How to resign

Resignations should always be done face-to-face. I've heard of people quitting by email, by voice mail, or just simply not showing up for work one day. These are great ways to burn bridges and destroy your reputation.

Request a few minutes of your boss' time. Have a brief letter prepared explaining that you have decided to resign and have accepted another job. It is not necessary to provide a detailed explanation of why you are leaving, although it might come up in your face-to-face meeting. Your letter should thank your employer for the opportunity they have given you to grow and expand your career, state the positive aspects of your experience with the company, and wish them well in the future. At this point, you should be thinking about maintaining good relations that will help you in years ahead. And never, never be critical of your employer.

Here is a sample resignation letter:

Dear Boss,

I would like to notify you that I have decided to resign from my position as Director of Logistics, effective October 15th.

Thank you for both the professional and personal development opportunities you have given to me during my time with the company. I have learned a great deal about this industry while working here and have totally enjoyed working with you and my co-workers.

I am pleased to help with the transition in any way I can. Best wishes to you.

Sincerely,

Your name

Notice period

If you have a written employment agreement, it should state the amount of notice period you are required to give your employer if you decide to resign. Be guided by this agreement and live up to the terms you agreed to when signing it, even if its enforceability is questionable. If you do not have a written agreement, you should still give reasonable notice. This could be anywhere from two weeks to three months, depending on your level of seniority, length of service, and scope of responsibilities.

In negotiating your notice period, think of your own needs last. Seek to create a balance between the needs of your current employer, whom you don't want to leave in the lurch, and your new employer, who likely wants you to start as soon as possible. Do your best to satisfy both interests.

Possible reactions

You should be ready for all possible reactions from your boss when you tell her you're leaving. In most cases, your boss will understand and be professional. She understands your reasons for leaving and agrees with your decision, even though it might be inconvenient for her. She knows it is the right move for you at this stage of your career, thanks you for your service to the company, and wishes you well. Too bad all resignations don't go as smoothly and professionally as that.

Unfortunately, sometimes the reaction is one of anger or disappointment. Your boss might be upset with you because of the possible disruption of work. She might realize how difficult it will be to locate a replacement. Or, she might even regard your quitting as a lack of loyalty to the company or her. Whatever the response, seek to calm these waters. Often these reactions are short-lived anyway, when the boss realizes the world is not ending just because you're leaving.

A word of caution: If you are leaving to join a direct competitor, you should expect that your boss will walk you right to the door. They will still have to honour any contractual obligations they have to you, such as vacation pay owed, but in all likelihood they will want you to leave right away. This can be awkward for everyone involved, so be prepared.

Counter-offers

It is possible too that your boss will try to convince you to stay with offers of higher pay, promotions, or increased responsibilities. This is a challenging response to deal with, particularly if you are not overly unhappy in your current job and like your co-workers.

However, these last-minute offers tend to be band-aid solutions and rarely address the underlying reasons for your original dissatisfaction. My experience is that most people who accept these offers and stay with their employer are looking for another job within a year.

Remember, work hard until your last day. The key here is to not burn any bridges with your current employer. So, keep your regular work hours and try to complete all outstanding projects you have on your desk. It also helps to prepare a detailed set of notes for your successor so he or she has a good idea about what work needs to be done.

Other tips to remember

- Never take anything that doesn't belong to you, particularly confidential or proprietary information like price lists or customer addresses.
- Always make sure you have your new offer in writing before you resign. You should not rely on verbal assurances as these can be easily rescinded.
- If you have a company cell phone or laptop and use these also for your personal use, make arrangements for new equipment of your own as you will have to turn in the company-owned equipment after you resign.
- Don't badmouth the company at any time. As others learn you are leaving, some disgruntled employees may try to engage in negative gossip sessions with you. Disassociate yourself from these people.

- And don't forget to notify and thank everybody you've been in contact with throughout your search. Let other employers, who may be considering you for a position know that you have accepted a new job. And advise networking contacts, recruiters, colleagues and friends with the same good news. Remember you may need this network down the road.

Ask Gerry

Q. Now that I have found a new job, what is the best way to conclude my search?

A. Once you've accepted your new position and resigned your current job, you should conclude your search in the same professional manner with which it was conducted. The relationships you developed throughout your search will continue to be important to you throughout your career. Let any other employers who may have been considering you for a position know that you have accepted an offer and thank them for their consideration and advice. You should also send information on your new work location to all those who supported your efforts. This includes all personal and business contacts, recruiters and other interested parties. Be sure to thank them all for their efforts and support. Finally, place the contact sheets, telephone numbers, email addresses, and any other relevant information from your search effort in a safe place for future reference. You never know when you might need them again.

Don't Pull a JetBlue

Steven Slater, a flight attendant with JetBlue Airlines, made national headlines in 2010 with his spectacular exit from an airplane (and his job) that had just landed at John F. Kennedy International Airport.

Here's what happened:

Flight 1052 from Pittsburgh had just landed and was taxiing along the runway to the terminal building. A passenger, whom Slater claims had been rude to him during the flight, stood up prematurely to retrieve luggage from the overhead bin. In the process, the passenger's luggage struck Slater in the head. He asked for an apology. The passenger refused. That's when Slater had his very public meltdown.

According to reports, Slater got on the plane's public address system and proceeded to tell off the entire planeload of passengers with an expletive-filled rant. He then activated the plane's escape chute, grabbed a beer from the beverage cart, and made a dazzling slide down the ramp, effectively ending his 20-year career in the airline industry.

One would think that Slater would be widely condemned for his actions and possibly endangering the safety of the passengers. Not so by the general public. His tirade became the subject of talk shows and newspapers for days, and he instantly became a folk hero to all those workers who have dreamed of telling off their boss as they go out in a blaze of glory. Similar actions became known as "pulling a JetBlue."

However, the authorities were not impressed. Slater was charged with criminal mischief, sentenced to one year of probation, ordered to pay $10,000 in damages to JetBlue, and instructed to complete a treatment program for mental health and alcohol problems. After being first suspended by the airline, he later resigned.

Section Six

The New Job

"Every time you get into a new job … you have an amazing opportunity in front of you. You get to play dumb for as long as people will allow you to play dumb. You get to ask all the dumb questions … and you get to make mistakes."

- Gary Cohn

Chapter 40

Strategies to Guarantee Success in Your New Job

**"You have brains in your head and feet in your shoes.
You can steer yourself any direction you choose."**

- Dr. Seuss

YOU WOULD THINK that boards of directors of major organizations would take plenty of time to make sure they hire the right CEO. Likewise, you would think the CEO – when he or she was hired – would have taken care to ensure they were the right candidate for the job. Apparently, that is not always the case. Yes, it's true: even CEOs fail.

According to studies, up to a third of Fortune 500 CEOs last less than three years. Yahoo, for example, had six CEOs in a five year window. (Between 2007 and 2012, Yahoo CEOs included Terry Semel, Jerry Yang, Carol Barty, Scott Thompson, Ross Levinsohn and Marissa Mayer.)

Most of you will not be at the CEO level. But that doesn't mean you can't learn from some of the fatal flaws they made that led to failure early in their tenure. In their book, "Why CEOs Fail: The 11 Behaviors That Can Derail Your Climb to the Top and How to Manage Them," David Dotlick and Peter Cairo list several reasons why CEOs fail. Not surprisingly, none have to do with their technical abilities. All have to do with personal quirks and characteristics which probably could have been avoided had someone had the nerve to confront the CEO and tell them what the problem was.

Dotlick and Cairo cited arrogance, aloofness, and a general distrust of others as three contributors to CEO failures on the job. They also noted that the failed CEOs demonstrated inconsistent behaviour and frequent mood swings, a need to sensationalize and exaggerate, and a resistance to making important decisions, as other factors that led to their downfalls.

Let's talk about you and your new job. I am sure that your initial reaction of getting the job was elation and excitement. But now that this initial reaction has worn off, it's time to start thinking about how you can start off your new job on the right foot.

For many people, concerns start to creep in. *Will I like my new job? What will the people be like? Will they like me? Can I do the work? Should I take courses to learn new skills? Will I fit into their organizational culture?*

Though starting a new job can be stressful, the transition does not have to be full of tension and anxiety. With careful planning and the right attitude, you can conclude a successful career change. In this final chapter, we will talk about proven strategies you can follow to ensure success in your new job.

Strategy #1
Prove what you told them in the interview

Whatever you said to the people who interviewed you, be sure that you demonstrate you can do it early on. For example, if you said you were good at web design, start to suggest ways the company's web site can be enhanced. Or if you claimed your strength is in motivating staff, start holding regular staff meetings or taking some other steps to prove it. All too often, candidates embellish their accomplishments in an interview. You don't want to be left in a situation where your performance falls short of your boss's expectations based on what you told them in the interview.

One way to do this is to pick off some "low hanging fruit." In a business context, low hanging fruit is a metaphor for doing the simplest or easiest work first or a target that is quick and easy to achieve. Doing so will help you build momentum and help establish your credibility early. Since these tasks do not require a lot of effort, it becomes an excellent strategy for you to employ during your first year to let others, especially your boss, know you are doing something.

Strategy #2
Make a positive first impression

Clearly, you made a good first impression in the interview. Now you have to carry this same attitude into your new job as all eyes will be on you as you begin. Here are a few strategies to follow:

- Think about how you dress. This might be a good time to revamp your wardrobe so you dress according to the company norm.

- Come to work early and stay late to demonstrate good work ethic and that you are not a "clock watcher."
- Adopt an attitude that you know almost nothing even if you were brought in to make a change. That means: ask good questions and listen more than you talk.
- Smile (a lot). There's nothing like a friendly face.
- Invite co-workers to lunch or coffee to learn about their jobs and build a personal relationship with them.
- Don't compare your old company to your new company, unless all your stories are about how much better your new company is, in which case it is fine to compare.
- Ask for help when you need it.
- Introduce yourself to everybody – this is no time to be shy.
- If you don't understand instructions from your boss, ask him to repeat them.

Strategy #3
Learn (and adopt) the behavioural norms

Every office has its own set of acceptable behaviours that employees are expected to follow. Failure to do so could cause irreparable damage to your long-term future with your new employer. Remember, you are the new kid on the block. You are the one who is expected to conform to these behaviours, not the other way around.

Some of these behavioural norms are clear-cut: If you take the last cup of coffee, make a fresh pot. Don't take other people's food from the fridge. And if you caused the paper jam in the printer, fix it.

Others however are less obvious. You will simply have to learn by watching and observing. Consider:

- Where do people eat? Is it okay to eat at your desk or does everyone eat in the lunchroom?
- How do people maintain their individual workstations? Is everyone's desk cleared off at end of the day or can work be left out?
- What about telephone etiquette? Is it okay to take the occasional personal call? How do other employees control their voice levels so they don't bother their neighbours?
- How do people speak to each other? What tone and language do they use?
- What do people wear to work? Pay special attention to "casual Fridays." Some people take the "casual" part too far.

- What about hours of work? Is it acceptable to come in 10 minutes late and stay 10 minutes longer at end of the day? Or does everyone work precisely 8:30 – 4:30?
- What are the meeting rules? Do they start right on time? Are people permitted to eat during staff meetings? What about bringing cell phones into meetings?
- Who cleans the dishes in the lunchroom? Is someone responsible for that task? Or does everyone clean their own?
- Is it okay to interrupt and walk into someone else's office if you have a question or problem? Or should a more formal approach be used?
- If you are meeting with someone and your boss calls, if it okay to interrupt the meeting and take the call?
- What email practices are followed? Is it appropriate to "cc" a large number of people even if they might not all consider the email important?

Strategy #4:
Determine the level of communication your boss wants

There are several relationships you will have to manage in your job but in most cases the essential one is with your new boss. In particular, it is important to establish the frequency with which she wishes to meet with you and the depth of information she requires about your work. For example, does she want to assign work to you and know everything you are doing? Is she okay with a daily meeting or weekly update?

Whatever it is, you should be prepared to adapt to her style. If she wants to know everything you do and you prefer a lot of freedom, don't resist it at the beginning. Give in to her way for the time being and build her trust level in you so she will give you more freedom over time.

Strategy #5
Understand the scope of your authority

Another useful piece of advice I give to new employees is to categorize your decision-making into three types.

- A *Level 1* decision is one you can make on your own without checking with your boss or telling him.
- A *Level 2* decision is one you can make on your own but one you should tell your boss after the fact that you made it so he will not be caught off-guard.

- A *Level 3* decision is one where you must receive approval from your boss before making it. Usually *Level 3* decisions are more strategic decisions and of greater importance and it is important that you gain approval beforehand.

It is best that you and your boss clearly understand which types of decisions fall where.

Strategy #6
Be respectful of the person you are replacing

When starting a new job new, particularly in a supervisory role, you should be aware of the person you have replaced. That person may have left for any number of reasons. Perhaps they retired, or were fired or just left to assume a new job somewhere else.

I spoke with Peter on the first anniversary of him taking over as Executive Director of a member-based association. A year earlier, Peter had taken over from Don, his predecessor, who was well respected and responsible for rescuing the organization from financial difficulties many years earlier. Peter said he was acutely aware that he and Don were very different people in terms of age, background, management style and even dress. Peter said, "I was very mindful there were staff who had worked with Don for the entire 11 years he had been there and who had become accustomed to his style."

Peter considered for a while whether he should change his style to match Don's. Or, should he just be himself? Ultimately, it was a "balance of both" said Peter, and that worked well. He was still able to be his authentic self yet respectful of relationships Don had with staff.

Strategy #7
Sort out the office politics

Every team, department, division or company has a different set of cultural norms and your failure to understand it can quickly lead to your downfall.

Take George (not his real name), a senior financial professional, who learned the hard way about office politics. "I entered a political nightmare where minds and opinions changed without notice," he told me. George had joined a family-owned business as their CFO, a newly created job, to oversee a controller and accounting supervisor, two long-term employees of the company. The company had been experiencing delays in implementing a new IT system and felt George had the necessary skills to get it done.

It didn't take long for problems to arise. While George was trying to get the project advanced, he was encountering difficulties in getting the controller and accounting supervisor to do their jobs in a different way, "a more efficient way," he said. Both held a lot of power (and sway) with the owner because they had been there so long. They also had great friendships with other staff members, friendships that carried on outside of work.

Here's how George described what happened: "After about two weeks on the job, the owner came into my office and said, 'The accounting supervisor and controller don't like you. Fix whatever you did or I will.' It turned out my staff could get me fired by just saying they didn't like me. I was walking on eggshells everywhere I went."

George then decided to confront the controller to discuss the problem. He asked him directly, "I heard you don't like me. What is the problem?" After more prodding, the controller finally opened up. He replied, "I have no problem with you professionally. You know what you are doing. You have more experience than me. Personally, you are a nice guy too. It's just the fact you are here. Before you arrived, I thought I was the CFO. You have my job. I found out you were coming in an email the Friday afternoon before you arrived in the position. It wasn't introduced or explained. You just came."

As George said to me, "I was the object of their anger, not the cause of their anger." Unfortunately there was nothing George could do to untangle the damage to his reputation and a couple of weeks later the owner fired him, claiming that he wasn't working well with staff.

In hindsight, George wishes he had been more aware of the "politics" within the company as he might have approached his work differently. While he thought he had the support of the owner, it turns out he did not. In particular, he learned two valuable lessons about work-related politics:

1. Certain people have more power than others, even if they lack formal title or position within the hierarchy.
2. Some people care so passionately about decisions at work that it leads to political behaviour as they try to get their way.

Whether you like it or not, office politics is a way of life in any organization and you need to understand and master it if you wish to succeed. Beyond understanding the formal organization and who has authority by virtue of their position, you should:

- Find out who the real influencers are – the people who can get things done even if they lack formal authority.
- Develop an understanding of the social networks that exist within the organization. Who gets along with whom? Who are the groups and cliques that connect? Which groups clash with each other?
- Don't align yourself with any one group; instead build your own social network by associating with many groups and networks across the entire organization.
- Most important, build your relationships on a firm foundation of trust, respect and high-quality work.

Strategy #8
Stay in touch with your old boss

Technically, this is not a strategy for being successful in your new job but it is a smart plan to follow just in case the new job doesn't work out. Assuming you followed my advice in earlier chapters and left on good terms, you can maintain a relationship with your old boss and past employer by:

- Sending a holiday card;
- Extending best wishes on their birthday;
- Updating them on major changes in your life such as marriage, new child, buying a house, or moving to a new location;
- Letting them know you've received a promotion or moved to a new job;
- Sending them articles of interest or forwarding any competitive intelligence you may have;
- Dropping in the office for a visit from time to time; and
- Staying in touch through Facebook, Twitter or LinkedIn .

If the new job doesn't work out, you might consider returning to your old employer. At a minimum, you may need them to provide a good reference should you decide to move on to something else.

Kristi's Story

Kristi Wenaus shares her experience transitioning from the private sector to a new job in the public sector.

> **Q. Tell us your story.**
> **A.** In 2007 I was given the opportunity to move from a private sector hospitality job into a government job with the department of tourism. I had been in the private sector of all my working life and did not

appreciate the cultural differences that existed between the two. In my mind, the subject matter was the same (sales and marketing in hotels = sales and marketing in tourism) so the work environment was sure to be the same.

How did you prepare for the new job?

I thought I had done all of the right things to prepare myself for my new role. I researched the department and the role before I started. I asked for the job descriptions for my new team so I could study them before I arrived. I re-read The First 90 Days by Michael Watkins to prepare myself for success. I even went so far as to meet with key stakeholders – who were former work colleagues of mine – to get a better sense of the scope and depth of the role. I walked in on Day 1 and was 100% sure I was prepared.

What happened when you arrived?

What I hadn't counted on was the fundamental difference in work culture that I was about to experience. Working in government is different. Not better or worse than the private sector – just different. I had heard this but didn't understand it and certainly didn't pay attention to it. Mostly I didn't appreciate how my actions and reactions during those critical first few months would affect my performance and my credibility.

How did you manage through this time?

I had great mentors and coaches who helped me see the unintended consequences of my early actions and swift decisions. I was hired to bring change to the department and to help them transition to a more private sector thinking. But I didn't take the time to appreciate why they worked the way they did. My mentors and coaches helped me understand that, in some instances, it needed to be the way it was and in fact worked well in the government setting. I was trying to change them when really it was me who needed to adapt.

What did you learn from this experience?

Organizational cultures exist for a reason. Sometimes it is necessary to change the internal culture for the better. However, I now know how important it is to really understand the reasons behind it first, before trying to blaze a new trail. It was a huge lesson that I will carry with me in each new job I start from this point forward.

* * *

Acknowledgements

First and foremost, I would like to thank the thousands of individuals I have had the pleasure to interview and coach over my many years as an executive recruiter and career coach.

In those meetings, you have shared personal details that described the challenges you have all faced in your search for the right career path. Your stories of success and failure helped me build the framework I outline in this book, and I have included many of these stories throughout the book. In some cases, you have allowed me to identify you and in others, I have respected your desire to remain anonymous. Because of your willingness to share, others will find the job search process a little bit easier. Thank you for your contributions.

I would also like to thank the people who provided me with feedback after reading my blogs, attending my workshops and viewing my television show. Your feedback is essential to my work. It has provided me with encouragement and inspiration, and also with opportunities to reflect and improve.

My editor, Dan Leger, was most helpful in shaping this book into its final form. Dan is an experienced journalist, writer and editor, having worked with The Canadian Press, the CBC and *The Chronicle Herald*. I am fortunate to have an editor with such a sharp eye and a sense of flow. Dan, I am pleased we connected and that you were willing to act as my editor.

My colleagues, Heather MacDonald and Lisa Kamperman, provided much-valued research, reviewed the many drafts from the perspective of the job seeker and provided valuable input into the final product. Heather and Lisa, thank you.

Monica MacDonald provided love, support and inspiration to me throughout the writing process. Even though she was busy writing her own book, she found time to proofread my work and offer constructive suggestions for improvement. Monica, you are a much more succinct writer than I am and I have learned from you. Thank you.

About the Author

Gerald Walsh is on a mission to help organizations find the right people and to help individuals find the right careers.

As one of Canada's most experienced executive recruiters, he has interviewed over 10,000 job candidates and completed thousands of executive search assignments at the management and professional levels. He has consulted with a wide range of organizations including owner-managed businesses, major corporations, governments and NGOs, not-for-profits and professional associations.

Gerry is an accomplished speaker and facilitator and he shares his deep experience by conducting keynote speeches and workshops for professional groups, industry associations, not-for-profit groups, universities and companies. His talks are engaging, practical, and rooted in real-life experiences.

He has written widely on careers, on managing people and leadership for professional publications and he blogs regularly on these topics. He is host of the cable TV series *Take This Job and Love It.*

Prior to founding his firm, Gerald Walsh Associates, Gerry worked in several industry sectors including manufacturing, technology and financial services. He is a professional accountant (CPA) and holds an MBA degree.

While Gerry has many volunteer and community interests, his passion is long-distance running. He is the founder of the Blue Nose Marathon in Halifax, Nova Scotia, has completed more than 25 full and half marathons and in his lifetime has run more than 30,000 miles.

Email	walsh@geraldwalsh.com
Website	www.geraldwalsh.com
Twitter	@Gerald_Walsh
LinkedIn	Gerry-Walsh (Halifax, Canada)

www.ingramcontent.com/pod-product-compliance
Lightning Source LLC
Chambersburg PA
CBHW082058210326
41521CB00032B/2468